REVISE AQA GCSE (9–1)
History
GERMANY, 1890–1945: DEMOCRACY AND DICTATORSHIP

REVISION
GUIDE AND WORKBOOK

Series Consultant: Harry Smith

Author: Kirsty Taylor

(handwritten margin notes)
S Understanding
Mindfulness
Livelihood
R Concentration
I Invention

Also available to support your revision:

Revise GCSE Study Skills Guide   9781292318875

The **Revise GCSE Study Skills Guide** is full of tried-and-trusted hints and tips for how to learn more effectively. It gives you techniques to help you achieve your best — throughout your GCSE studies and beyond!

Revise GCSE Revision Planner   9781292318868

The **Revise GCSE Revision Planner** helps you to plan and organise your time, step-by-step, throughout your GCSE revision. Use this book and wall chart to mastermind your revision.

> **For the full range of Pearson revision titles across KS2, 11+, KS3, GCSE, Functional Skills, AS/A Level and BTEC visit:**
> www.pearsonschools.co.uk/revise

Contents

. . . .

A small bit of small print
AQA publishes Sample Assessment Material and the Specification on its website. This is the official content and this book should be used in conjunction with it. The questions and revision tasks in this book have been written to help you revise the skills you may need for your assessment. Remember: the real assessment may not look like this.

Ruling Germany

In 1871, the German-speaking states in Europe united to become a new country: Germany. The king of the largest and most powerful state, Prussia, became the **Kaiser** (Emperor) of Germany. Many of Prussia's ideas were very influential in the government of the new country.

The constitution of the German Empire, 1890

> Hereditary means passed from parent to child.

Kaiser

A **hereditary** monarch (also King of Prussia) as Head of State.

- Appointed the Chancellor.
- Could dismiss the Chancellor and/or the Chancellor's ministers.
- Power to dissolve the Reichstag.
- Commander of the armed forces.
- In charge of foreign policy.

The army

- Swore an oath of allegiance to the Kaiser.
- Highest ranks advised the Kaiser and therefore could play a political role.
- Officers were from upper classes, usually right wing and politically conservative.
- Depended on the Reichstag for funding but only every five years.

Chancellor (Chief minister)

- Responsible only to the Kaiser.
- Appointed his own ministers to help him make government policies.
- Led the Bundesrat, and proposed topics and laws to be debated.
- Could choose to ignore the decisions of the Reichstag.

Bundesrat (Federal Council)

- Made up of representatives from the 25 state governments of Germany but dominated by Prussia.
- Consulted with the Kaiser and Chancellor over government policies.
- Proposed laws that were then sent to the Reichstag. It then had to approve the laws passed by the Reichstag.

Reichstag (Parliament)

- Made up of members elected by universal male suffrage (all men over 25 years of age) in a secret ballot every three years, or sooner if dismissed by the Kaiser.
- Passed, amended or rejected laws proposed by the Bundesrat/Chancellor.
- Could pass or reject a grant to fund the military every five years.

Prussian militarism

Prussia had often been threatened by other countries so believed strongly in **militarism** (the idea that a country should have strong armed forces). This meant:

- a large army in proportion to its population size
- high government spending on maintaining the army at all times
- a strong culture of service and absolute loyalty to the king from the army
- the army was respected and admired by Prussian society.

Influence of Prussian militarism

As Prussia was the dominant state within Germany, its militarism became very influential. Also, as the Prussian army was experienced, well equipped and well led, it was used as the basis for the German army. The army Generals had great influence in Germany's government, just as before, when Prussia was an independent state and they were advisers to the Kaiser. They had strong views on foreign policy, and would play an increasingly important role in government under Kaiser Wilhelm II, until they were in complete control of Germany in the final years of the First World War.

Now try this

Define the following terms: Kaiser; Reichstag; Chancellor; Prussia; militarism.

1

Kaiser Wilhelm II

Kaiser Wilhelm II had a lot of power, so his character, aims and beliefs were very important. However, he could not do whatever he wanted. The Chancellor and other ministers could shape policy. Also, his reign saw a growth in parliamentary democracy, which meant it could be difficult to get the Reichstag to pass legislation.

Kaiser Wilhelm II

Became Kaiser in 1888, aged 29.

Grandson of Queen Victoria and related to many other European monarchs.

Passionate and energetic, but could be unstable; had a violent temper.

Very determined to get his own way.

Before becoming Kaiser, spent much of his time in the army and was very interested in all things military.

Believed it was his destiny to rule.
Unlike previous Kaisers, he wanted a very active, hands-on role in ruling Germany, and had little regard for the Reichstag.

Wilhelm's aims and beliefs

A strong believer in militarism.
He held the army in very high regard. He frequently consulted his army generals and valued their advice. Indeed, they often directed policy, especially foreign policy, far more than his ministers, Reichstag or Bundesrat.

Wanted Germany to rival Britain as the most powerful country in the world. He wanted to build an overseas empire to add to Germany's wealth and power – pushed for **Weltpolitik** (world policy).

Chancellors under Kaiser Wilhelm

- In theory, the Kaiser had a great deal of power as he could remove the Chancellor, ministers and the Reichstag when he wanted. However, Kaisers before Wilhelm II had not done so. They were happy for Chancellor Bismarck (who had held the office since 1871) to rule for them, which he did effectively.

- One of Wilhelm II's first actions as Kaiser was to dismiss Bismarck. He did not want anyone to be more powerful than himself and disagreed with Bismarck's **Realpolitik** (policies based on realism rather than idealism). He appointed Caprivi as Chancellor, but after Caprivi proposed some social reforms he too was dismissed in 1894.

- After this, Wilhelm II chose Chancellors and other ministers who had the same aims and beliefs as he did.

For more about social reforms, see page 3.

The growth of parliamentary government

- Wilhelm II did not have complete power as Germany had an elected Reichstag, which was needed to pass legislation.

- Wilhelm II could dismiss the Reichstag (which he often did), but the elections were freely held so he could not directly influence the vote.

- Before 1890 political parties had started to develop and this continued under Wilhelm II's rule. This meant Reichstag members were loyal to other members of their party and not always totally loyal to the Kaiser.

- In reality, these political parties had little direct power to change things, but they acted as pressure groups on the government and influenced public opinion.

The growth of socialism and the Social Democratic Party (SDP) was particularly concerning to Kaiser Wilhelm II. The SPD frequently voted against the legislation the Kaiser wanted.

Kaiser Wilhelm II's chancellors

- Caprivi 1890–94
- Hohenlohe 1894–1900
- Budlow 1900–09
- Bethmann Hollweg 1909–17

Now try this

For each of the following, write a sentence explaining what, if any, influence they had on Kaiser Wilhelm II:
(a) army generals; (b) the Reichstag; (c) his Chancellors.

Industrialisation and socialism

Under Kaiser Wilhelm II, Germany rapidly industrialised. This created wealth but only for a few. A growing number of industrial workers were becoming dissatisfied, leading to the growth of socialism. Industrialisation, therefore, brought great benefits to Germany but also created difficulties for the Kaiser.

Industrialisation

Industrialisation in Germany began before 1890 but between 1890 and 1913 the speed of industrial growth was astonishing. This was partly due to rapid population growth, which provided workers as well as consumers.

 Industrialisation is the process of moving from a largely agricultural economy to one based on manufacturing industrial goods.

👍 Traditional industries grew rapidly. Coal production rivalled Britain's by 1914. Iron and steel production was better.

👍 More coal, iron and steel helped to build and fuel railways, trains and ships, aiding communications and trade.

👍 By 1914, Germany was also out-producing the rest of Europe in 'newer' industries such as electrical goods and chemicals.

👍 Generally, people became wealthier and standards of living improved.

👎 Industrialisation was accompanied by rapid urbanisation as people moved to towns and cities for work. Living conditions were poor; outbreaks of diseases such as cholera were common.

👎 Although most people shared in increased prosperity and unemployment was very low, the gaps between rich and poor grew wider.

👎 Agricultural production did not increase at the same rate so more food was imported. Food was expensive.

👎 High rates of immigration, mostly from Eastern Europe, provided more workers but fuelled social problems as hatred of 'foreigners' (and especially **anti-Semitism** – prejudice against Jewish people) grew.

The growth of socialism

In Germany, **socialism** (the idea that the profits from industry should be shared equally between everyone in society) had been growing alongside industrialisation since unification in 1871 and continued to grow in popularity after 1890. Socialism was greatly feared by the ruling and middle classes. It became an increasing problem for the Kaiser because he needed the Reichstag to pass new laws.

The Social Democratic Party (SPD)

The **SPD** (a political party that wanted more socialist policies and rights for workers in Germany) attracted increasing support from voters. In every election from 1890, the SPD won the most votes but it was not until 1912 that it held the most seats in the Reichstag. SPD members of the Reichstag consistently voted against some of the Kaiser's desired laws. He could dismiss the Reichstag, which he did on several occasions, but the same or new members of the SPD were voted back in again.

Social reform

There were some efforts to meet the worker's concerns:

- In 1891, employing children under 13 years old, women working over 11 hours a day and businesses operating on a Sunday were all banned.

- Throughout the period, old age pensions and welfare provisions for those too ill or injured to work (introduced in 1890) were improved.

- After 1900, industrial courts to settle disputes between workers and their employers were made compulsory in towns of over 20,000 people.

Many of these reforms were put forward by Chancellor Caprivi, who believed that they would ease the pressure from socialism. However, Kaiser Wilhelm II thought Caprivi was too socialist and dismissed him in 1894.

Now try this

Give an example of how industrialisation caused difficulties for Kaiser Wilhelm II.

3

The Navy Laws

Increasing the German armed forces was a central part of Weltpolitik. Wilhelm II was convinced that building a powerful navy was vitally important. From 1898 to 1912 a series of Navy Laws were passed that extended the size and power of the German navy. As well as worrying some other countries, the laws had a profound impact within Germany, and caused further difficulties for Wilhelm II.

Timeline

1897 Kaiser appointed Admiral von Tirpitz Navy Secretary

1898 German Navy League established First Naval Law – approval to increase the size of the navy by seven battleships, taking the total to 19

1900 Second Naval Law – approval to double the size of the navy to 38 battleships

1904 Entente Cordiale agreement between Britain and France

1906 Third Naval Law – another six battleships
Britain launches the first dreadnought
Amendments to the Naval Laws; some of the battleships are changed to dreadnoughts

1907 Triple Entente between Britain, France and Russia

1908 Further amendments to Naval Laws approving 21 dreadnoughts

1912 Further amendments to Naval Laws further increasing the size of the fleet

Reasons for the Navy Laws

Partly due to the influence of his new Navy Secretary, Alfred von Tirpitz, Wilhelm pushed his government to increase the size and power of the navy. Wilhelm was convinced that it would:

- lead to further industrial growth
- protect and potentially increase Germany's empire
- be a great symbol of Germany's power in the world
- rival the Royal Navy of Britain.

The Navy League

A patriotic group which aimed to popularise the navy and naval expansion and represented the navy as a symbol of German greatness. It was supported by many industrialists and soon had over 200,000 members. Tirpitz helped set it up and it certainly helped him get the First and Second Naval Laws passed by the Reichstag with substantial majorities.

The domestic importance of the Navy Laws

Britain's response to the Navy Laws helped create a greater fear within Germany which generated support for the Kaiser's other policies.

Helped industries and businesses by creating more work and employing more people.

Created conflict between the Kaiser and army leaders who argued that the army should have the money allocated to the navy (though spending on the army increased as well).

The huge cost was born by raising taxes (mostly indirect taxes which hit the lower classes more) and borrowing money.

Domestic is something within that country, as opposed to foreign or international.

The SPD was very opposed to the Navy Laws (mostly due to the expense). This won them some support but also helped the Kaiser present the SPD as the unpatriotic 'enemy' within.

The Navy Laws encouraged patriotism and nationalism and therefore helped win support for the policy of Weltpolitik.

SMS *Westfalen*, a German battleship built due to Navy Laws

Now try this

Give **two** reasons why many Germans approved of the Navy Laws and **two** reasons why some (including some government ministers) were opposed to them.

The difficulties of ruling Germany

Unlike his predecessors, Kaiser Wilhelm II played a central and very active role in ruling Germany for most of his reign. He had very strong ideas about what he wanted to achieve but, despite his huge power, he faced difficulties in ruling Germany and realising the policies he wanted.

Growth of parliamentary government

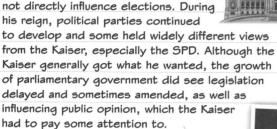

Although the Kaiser could dismiss the Reichstag whenever he wanted, he did need it to pass legislation and could not directly influence elections. During his reign, political parties continued to develop and some held widely different views from the Kaiser, especially the SPD. Although the Kaiser generally got what he wanted, the growth of parliamentary government did see legislation delayed and sometimes amended, as well as influencing public opinion, which the Kaiser had to pay some attention to.

For a reminder about the growth of parliamentary government, look at page 2.

Prussian militarism

The Kaiser was a keen supporter of militarism and this played a part in leading him into conflict with other major European powers. It also caused him problems domestically in two main areas:

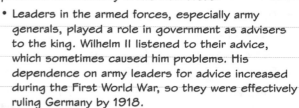

- Leaders in the armed forces, especially army generals, played a role in government as advisers to the king. Wilhelm II listened to their advice, which sometimes caused him problems. His dependence on army leaders for advice increased during the First World War, so they were effectively ruling Germany by 1918.

- Maintaining and growing the size of the army were very expensive and the Kaiser needed the Reichstag's approval for military spending.

For a reminder about Prussian militarism, look at page 1.

Kaiser Wilhelm II and the difficulties of ruling Germany

For a reminder about the Navy Laws, look at page 4.

For a reminder about industrialisation, look at page 3.

The Navy Laws

The Kaiser pushed for the navy to be greatly expanded and was therefore an enthusiastic supporter of the Navy Laws, but they still caused him some difficulties:

- Some members of the Reichstag and others in society were very opposed to the Navy Laws mostly because of the huge sums of money needed to enact them.

- Army leaders disapproved of the Navy Laws because they believed the navy was growing at the expense of the army, which brought them into conflict with the Kaiser.

Industrialisation

As well as bringing wealth to Germany, which increased its power in Europe, industrialisation brought the Kaiser some problems:

- Industrialisation created many social problems, especially poor living and working conditions and conflict between workers due to immigration which the Kaiser and his government were expected to solve.

- Industrialisation led to the working classes taking a greater interest in politics which led to a growth in socialism.

Socialism

The Kaiser, along with most of the ruling and middle classes, greatly feared socialism and the potential rise of workers to overthrow the existing social, economic and political system. Its growth led to a major difficulty for the Kaiser as socialists formed their own political party – the Social Democratic Party – which attracted increasing popular support throughout his reign, gaining more and more seats in the Reichstag. The SPD frequently made it difficult for the Kaiser to get the legislation he wanted.

For a reminder about socialism, look at page 3.

Now try this

Which of the Kaiser's difficulties in ruling Germany would have worried him the most? Explain why.

War weariness and economic problems

When the First World War broke out in August 1914, Germany was a wealthy nation and most Germans enjoyed a good standard of living. Many Germans were proud of their country and confident of a quick victory. By 1918, the situation was very different.

War weariness in Germany

There had been a small number of protests against the war in Germany since 1915 but by the middle of 1918, many German civilians had had enough of the war.

- Thousands of men had been killed and many thousands more injured.
- There were serious food shortages in Germany, as well as other economic problems.
- They were exhausted with working the long hours demanded for the war effort.

The Battle of the Somme (July–November 1916) was one of the bloodiest of the war. At least 150,000 Germans were killed.

War weariness in the military

As the war went on, more soldiers became disheartened with the war, although most remained confident of victory. However, in the summer of 1918 disillusionment became worse and desertions from the army dramatically increased as allied forces, reinforced by US troops, won battle after battle. Sailors in the navy were also becoming increasingly unhappy. This led to **mutiny** (rebellion) in October 1918, which in turn led to the Kaiser's abdication and Germany's defeat.

To learn more about Germany's defeat in the First World War, look at page 7.

Economic problems in Germany, 1918

The British Royal Navy was preventing food supplies reaching Germany by sea. By 1918, there were serious food shortages. Many people were malnourished and surviving on turnips and bread.

As the Royal Navy prevented ships from reaching Germany, there were non-food shortages, such as raw materials needed by some industries and medicines.

Many working-class Germans had their wages restricted during the war, so were worse off in 1918 than they had been before the war. In contrast, a few businesses had made vast amounts of money for their owners, which made many workers angry.

Germany had printed more money to finance the war. However, it didn't have the gold to support it, so the value of the German mark was much lower in 1918 than it had been in 1914.

Many middle- and upper-class Germans had helped to pay for the war through buying war bonds from the government. The government would need to repay this money to keep their support.

Germany had lent money to its allies to help their war effort. However, these countries had serious economic problems themselves, so could not repay their debts.

The Allied blockade of Germany (which prevented goods entering or leaving) caused great suffering, with people reduced to scavenging. According to German statistics at the time nearly 763,000 Germans died of starvation during and immediately after the war. Another 150,000 died in the flu pandemic of autumn 1918.

As more soldiers died and others were too injured to work, the state had to support an increasing number of families through war pensions.

Germany had bought food and other goods from other countries on credit. These debts would have to be repaid.

As well as the reduction in manufactured goods to sell, trade had been severely disrupted by the war, and national income was two-thirds less than it had been before the war.

With the loss of workers and a focus on producing equipment for the war effort, industrial production in 1918 was about one-third less than before the war.

Now try this

Which **three** aspects of Germany's economic problems in 1918 do you think would have worried ordinary Germans the most? Explain your answer.

Germany's defeat

As the war continued, the power of Germany's military leaders grew. They made all the major decisions, sometimes without consulting the Kaiser. By 1918, Wilhelm II was little more than a figurehead.

What led to Germany's defeat and the end of the monarchy?

> On 29 September 1918, Field Marshal **Hindenburg** and General **Ludendorff** informed Kaiser Wilhelm II and members of the Bundesrat and Reichstag that Germany would never be able to win the war. They advised negotiating with the allies for an **armistice** (formal agreement to end the war) based on US President Wilson's conditions for peace, which demanded greater democracy in Germany.

> On 3 October 1918, Kaiser Wilhelm II appointed a liberal man, Prince Max of Baden, as Chancellor and reluctantly transferred some of his powers to the Reichstag. A new government was formed, which took back control of Germany from the army leaders. This wasn't enough. President Wilson demanded Kaiser Wilhelm II should **abdicate** (give up his throne). In Germany popular demonstrations against the war increased.

> On 28 October, sailors in the navy stationed at Kiel in Northern Germany refused to follow orders to attack the British Royal Navy. The mutiny quickly spread to other ports where more sailors refused to follow their orders.

> The naval mutinies triggered other uprisings across Germany. Some workers went on strike and held large protests in the streets. Some soldiers refused to restore order. Within days, some local authorities had been overthrown; councils of workers and soldiers were running many towns and cities. Meanwhile, at the front, soldiers were deserting.

> Kaiser Wilhelm II fled to the army headquarters in Spa, Belgium, on 9 November. Ministers tried to persuade him to abdicate. He refused. Army leaders then withdrew their support and on 10 November he fled to the Netherlands.

> Germany was then declared a republic by Philipp Scheidemann, a leading member of the SPD, the largest party in the Reichstag. The November Revolution had begun. SPD leader **Friedrich Ebert** was made temporary leader of the country.

> On 10 November, Ebert formed the **Council of People's Representatives** with leading socialists, to run the country until elections could be held. The army leaders agreed to work with the new government.

> On 11 November, the new government signed the armistice. The First World War was over and Germany had been defeated.

The 'stab in the back' legend

Throughout the war, many Germans believed it when they were told that Germany was winning. Although many were relieved the war was over, defeat was an unexpected shock. This led to the idea that the German army had been 'stabbed in the back' by politicians. Many historians believe that army leaders were largely responsible for this idea as, despite being in charge in 1918, they forced politicians to seek peace and left negotiations to them. They also never admitted defeat. As Germany had never been invaded, some found defeat difficult to accept.

The Treaty of Versailles

Many Germans found the peace terms totally unacceptable. The new government had little choice but to sign the **Treaty of Versailles** (the official agreement that ended the war) but this made it unpopular. Terms included:

- accepting that Germany started the war (the War Guilt clause)
- paying **reparations** (financial amends)
- loss of land in Europe and all overseas colonies
- placing severe limits on the German military
- preventing Germany joining with Austria.

Now try this

Give **three** reasons for the Kaiser's abdication in November 1918.

Post-war problems

The post-war problems grew, resulting in the **hyperinflation** crisis of 1923.

Reparations

- By signing the Treaty of Versailles, the German government had agreed to pay reparations to the countries who had won the war.
- In 1921, the amount was decided: £6.6 billion marks over 66 years. This was a massive amount, especially considering Germany's huge economic problems. It increased German hatred of the Treaty and the government that had signed it.

> For a reminder about Germany's economic problems, look at page 6.

- Moreover, Germany's inability to make the payments led to two huge crises in 1923: the invasion of the Ruhr and hyperinflation.

Hyperinflation

When the price of goods increases it is called inflation; when it increases spectacularly, it is called hyperinflation.

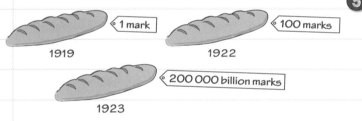

1 mark — 1919
100 marks — 1922
200 000 billion marks — 1923

The invasion of the Ruhr and hyperinflation

1. In 1921 Germany managed to pay the first reparations instalment but in December 1922 Germany announced it could not afford to pay the second instalment.

2. In January 1923, French and Belgian troops invaded the Ruhr (part of Germany near France) taking control of all factories and mines. They took raw materials, machinery and manufactured goods back to France and Belgium in place of reparation payments due.

3. The German government urged **passive resistance** (non-violent opposition), so workers in the Ruhr went on strike. Some of them damaged goods and machinery.

4. French and Belgian soldiers arrested, expelled and even killed some striking workers. French and Belgian workers were brought in to replace the strikers.

5. The German economy was badly hit. It didn't have the produce from the Ruhr to sell (80% of its coal, iron and steel was in the region). It also had to pay the striking workers. The government decided to print more money, which led to hyperinflation. By November 1923, the German mark was worthless.

The effects of hyperinflation

Negative effects

- Some people could not afford essentials like bread.
- Wages rose, but not as quickly as prices.
- Some businesses went bankrupt. (Those that made money took over the struggling ones.)
- People with fixed or monthly incomes, such as pensioners, suffered most.
- Savings became worthless. This affected the middle classes most.
- People blamed the Weimar government, which made it even more unpopular.

Positive effects

- Farmers benefited, as they were paid more for food.
- Some people and businesses could pay off loans and mortgages.
- Fixed rents for rooms or shops became very cheap.
- Foreign visitors could buy more for their money.

Now try this

Make a list of all the ways in which Germany was affected by hyperinflation.
Include the groups or types of person most affected.

The effects of hyperinflation on Germany are important for understanding various topics, so make sure you revise them.
- Remember that middle-class people were worst affected.
- Include positive and negative effects of hyperinflation in your list.

Had a look ☐   Nearly there ☐   Nailed it! ☐

Weimar
democracy

The Weimar government

Ebert and the Council of People's Representatives tried to establish order in the weeks and months after the armistice. Elections were held in January 1919 and the new National Assembly set to work on a new constitution for Germany. On 31 July 1919, the Weimar Republic officially began.

The Weimar Constitution

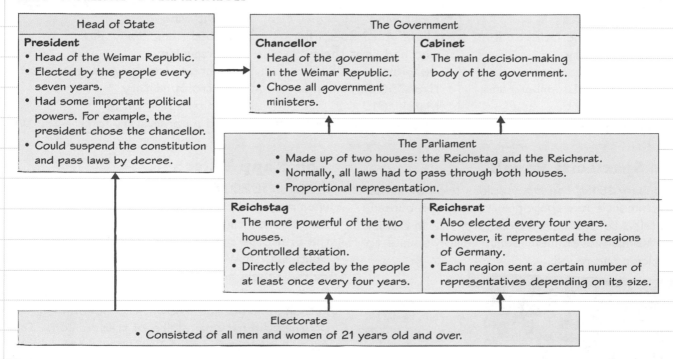

Head of State

President
- Head of the Weimar Republic.
- Elected by the people every seven years.
- Had some important political powers. For example, the president chose the chancellor.
- Could suspend the constitution and pass laws by decree.

The Government

Chancellor
- Head of the government in the Weimar Republic.
- Chose all government ministers.

Cabinet
- The main decision-making body of the government.

The Parliament
- Made up of two houses: the Reichstag and the Reichsrat.
- Normally, all laws had to pass through both houses.
- Proportional representation.

Reichstag
- The more powerful of the two houses.
- Controlled taxation.
- Directly elected by the people at least once every four years.

Reichsrat
- Also elected every four years.
- However, it represented the regions of Germany.
- Each region sent a certain number of representatives depending on its size.

Electorate
- Consisted of all men and women of 21 years old and over.

Elections in January 1919

Despite the chaos in Germany, there was a very high turnout in the elections for the new National Assembly on 19 January 1919. Moderate parties won the most votes:
- The SPD won 40%
- The Centre Party won 20%.

Ebert became the first President of Weimar Germany. Scheidemann became the Chancellor.

Strengths and weaknesses of the Weimar constitution

Strengths	Weaknesses
• Proportional representation made sure small parties had a fair share of seats. • Women able to vote as well as men. • Voting age reduced from 25 to 21. • No one group or person could have too much power. • There was an election for president every seven years. • Central government was more powerful than before, but local government still retained power in the regions. • The Reichsrat could regulate the power of the Reichstag by delaying new laws.	• Proportional representation led to coalition governments that were unstable, or found it difficult to have strong policies and often fell apart. • Lack of strong government led to weakness in a crisis that ended up with the president passing laws without the prior consent of the Reichstag. Article 48 of the constitution enabled the president to do this. • It was not the choice of the people so was not that popular.

Now try this

Describe **three** differences between the constitution of the German Empire in 1890 and the Weimar Constitution of 1919.

9

Change and unrest, 1919–23

The new government faced challenges from extreme political parties that did not agree with the democratic approach being established in the Weimar Republic.

The Spartacists	The Freikorps	The National Socialist German Workers' Party (Nazis)
• Left-wing • Came from the Independent Socialist Party • Had Soviet backing • Led by Rosa Luxemburg and Karl Liebknecht • Based in Berlin	• Right-wing • Made up of ex-soldiers who had kept their weapons • Had 250 000 men in March 1919 • Organised by regular army	• Right-wing • Hated democracy and communism • Wanted strong government with a strong military • Led by Adolf Hitler • Had a paramilitary force – the SA

The Spartacist Revolt

In January 1919, the Spartacists took over the government's newspaper and telegraph bureau, and tried to organise a general strike in Berlin. The Weimar government sent Freikorps units to put down the revolt.

There was street fighting in Berlin for several days before the revolt ended and Spartacist leaders were shot.

The Kapp Putsch

In March 1920, Freikorps troops, fearing unemployment, decided to march on Berlin. Ebert asked the head of the army to resist the Freikorps but he refused. A nationalist politician, Dr Wolfgang Kapp, was put in charge by the rebels and the Weimar government fled Berlin. In order to stop the rebels, or Kapp Putsch as it became known, the government organised a national strike of trade unions. This caused such chaos that Kapp could not rule Germany and was forced to flee. The Weimar ministers returned.

The Munich Putsch

For a reminder about the economic crisis of 1923, look at page 8.

The economic crisis of 1923 plus the success of Mussolini's Fascist Party in Italy in 1922, led to – **Hitler's Nazi Party** trying to seize power in Germany.

The Putsch failed because of lack of support. Hitler was imprisoned and the Nazi Party was banned. However, in the long term there were some positive consequences for Hitler and the Nazi Party:

- Hitler used his trial to publicise his views. He was given only a short prison term and released after nine months.
- While in prison he wrote *Mein Kampf* ('My Struggle'), a book outlining his political and racial ideas that became a bestseller.
- The failure of the Putsch made Hitler rethink the party's tactics. He realised he would have to win support through elections. The ban on the party was lifted by 1925.

The events of the Putsch

Timeline

8 November 1923
Hitler, with 600 SA, entered a beer hall in Munich where the Bavarian government was meeting. At gunpoint, Hitler forced government leaders to support him. Röhm took over local police and army headquarters. Ludendorff, behind Hitler's back, let the government leaders go.

9 November 1923
Hitler, 1000 SA and 2000 volunteer supporters marched on Munich town centre to declare Hitler President of Germany. They were met by state police. Someone opened fire and there was chaos. Ludendorff, Röhm and Streicher were arrested.

11 November 1923
Hitler was found hiding at a friend's house and was arrested.

Now try this

Describe the role of the Freikorps in the Kapp Putsch and the Spartacist Revolt.

Economic developments, 1924–29

Between 1924 and 1929, Germany recovered from the crisis of 1923 but there were still significant weaknesses in its economy. This period is known as the Stresemann era, due to the role in the recovery played by Gustav Stresemann, who was Chancellor August–November 1923, then Foreign Minister until 1929.

Rentenmark

☑ In November 1923, Stresemann set up the Rentenbank and issued a new currency called the Rentenmark.

☑ Supply of these notes was tightly controlled. Their value was tied to the price of gold so it had real value. This encouraged more public confidence.

☑ In August 1924 the Reichsbank was given control of this new currency. It was renamed the Reichsmark. Hyperinflation was over.

The Reichsmark provided a much stronger basis for the recovery of jobs and businesses, but it could not bring back the losses experienced in the hyperinflation crisis.

International loans after the First World War

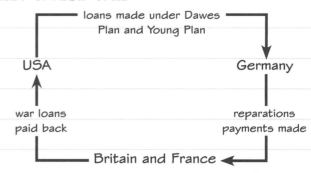

loans made under Dawes Plan and Young Plan

USA → Germany

war loans paid back ↑ reparations payments made ↓

Britain and France

The Dawes Plan, 1924

In 1924, Charles Dawes, an American banker, designed a plan so Germany could pay its reparations.

- Instalments were temporarily reduced to £50 million a year.
- US banks agreed to make loans to German industry. The Allies felt more confident that they would get their reparations payments.

Gustav Stresemann (far left) at the London conference in 1924, where the Dawes Plan was agreed.

Young Plan, 1929

In August 1929, a committee, set up by the Allies and led by an American banker called Owen Young, proposed a plan.

👍 The Young Plan reduced the total reparations debt from £6.6 billion to £2 billion.

👍 The payments could be made over a longer time, up until 1988.

👍 Lower reparations meant lower taxes for German people.

👎 There was a lot of opposition, especially from the extreme political parties, like the Nazis, who felt it was extending the burden for future generations.

Improvements in the economy

The Weimar Republic's economy improved because:

👍 industrial output doubled by 1928 and finally passed pre-First World War levels

👍 employment and trade increased.

However, there were still problems:

👎 The extreme political parties were completely against Germany paying the reparations at all.

👎 The economic recovery depended on American loans, so remained fragile.

Now try this

Write a paragraph to explain how the German economy was still vulnerable, despite improvements.

International agreements

As well as the Dawes and Young Plans, Stresemann negotiated several more international agreements between 1925 and 1929 which were to have a positive impact on recovery in Germany.

Impact of international agreements

The international agreements had a significant impact and helped Germany recover from post-war problems. The agreements:

- strengthened the confidence of the German people in the Weimar Republic
- improved Germany's relationship with other countries, therefore gaining their support and help – for example, economically
- helped economic recovery and reduced the hardships of the German people
- increased support for the moderate political parties who had made the agreements and reduced support for extremist parties such as the Nazis and Communists, therefore improving political stability.

However, problems remained and not everyone was pleased with the agreements.

League of Nations

This was a new international body that hoped to discuss world problems in order to avoid resorting to war. It was set up in 1920 but Germany was initially excluded. In 1926, they were invited to join and become a member of the council.

Why was it a success for Germany?

- It showed that Germany's views counted.
- It boosted the confidence held by most Germans in the Weimar government.

Locarno Pact 1925

This was an agreement between Germany, Britain, France, Italy and Belgium. In it:

- Germany agreed to its new border with France, improving relations with the French
- the Allies and Germany agreed to the permanent demilitarisation of the Rhineland
- German membership of the League of Nations was up for discussion.

Why was it a success for Germany?

- It improved relations with France with the border agreement.
- It was not imposed on Germany, unlike the Treaty of Versailles.
- It increased the status and popularity of the Weimar Republic.
- It helped boost confidence in more moderate political parties.

Kellogg–Briand Pact 1928

This was an agreement between 62 nations. It committed countries to avoiding the use of war to achieve foreign policy objectives.

Why was it a success for Germany?

- It showed that Germany was once again a major power.
- It showed that moderate political parties could build Germany's strength internationally.
- It increased public confidence in how Germany was being led.

Limits to recovery

The German recovery was not total and there were still some problematic areas.

- ✓ Some sectors of the economy (such as agriculture) saw little recovery.
- ✓ The economy was dependent on loans.
- ✓ Some Germans didn't like the agreements.
- ✓ The hated terms of the Treaty of Versailles were still in place.
- ✓ Extremist parties had not disappeared.

Now try this

Give **three** ways in which international agreements helped Germany. Then give **three** ways in which they did not help or were unpopular.

Remember to include the Dawes Plan and Young Plan when considering international agreements. For a reminder of these, look at page 11.

Weimar culture

The extent of recovery in Germany can be seen by the flourishing of culture between 1924 and 1929. The main driving force in art and cinema was the movement called **Expressionism**. This was radically different from before, when the emphasis was on recreating beautiful things from nature and traditional stories.

Art

Weimar artists painted everyday life so that everyone could have access to their art. They wanted to make art that commented on problems in German society, or to make people think. Their style of work was called Expressionism, which was concerned with raw emotion, the seedier side of everyday life and confronting the disaster of the First World War. Artists like Otto Dix and George Grosz were influential to the movement, as was Paul Klee.

Cinema

Films became popular all over the world in the 1920s. Expressionism flourished in film-making, particularly in Weimar Germany due to fewer restrictions. Some German films were very new and exciting in how they challenged traditional cinema.

Expressionism is an abstract style of art where feelings and emotions are more important than showing physical reality.

A famous and very popular German actress of the time was Marlene Dietrich. Here she is in the film *The Woman One Longs For*, directed by Curtis Bernhardt in 1929.

The films below were marked by dark shadows, dramatic lighting and grotesque characters.

'Cave Flowers' by Paul Klee, 1926. Klee taught at the Bauhaus school.

Science Fiction
Metropolis
Directed by
Fritz Lang

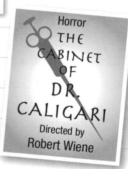

Horror
THE CABINET OF DR. CALIGARI
Directed by
Robert Wiene

Ghost story
The Cat and the Canary
Directed by
Paul Leni

Architecture

New designers and architects challenged traditional ideas and practices in building and interiors.

The Bauhaus school was set up in Weimar, in 1919, by the architect Walter Gropius.

Gropius wanted to bring together all the disciplines (art, architecture, design, typography, sculpture, and so on.).

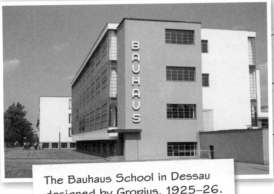

The Bauhaus School in Dessau designed by Gropius, 1925–26.

The school attracted many talented artists and designers.

Their ideas challenged traditional styles that had been popular before the war.

Their approaches looked radical compared to what had come before.

Now try this

What did Weimar art, cinema and architecture have in common?

Growth of extremism, 1928–32

By 1929 Germany had made great progress in recovering from the economic and social problems caused by the First World War. However, the Wall Street Crash in October 1929 led to the Great Depression, which caused huge economic problems. Extremist parties grew in popularity again.

The impact of the Depression

Bank panic, Germany 1931

Wall Street Crash, USA, October 1929
US companies lost billions of dollars in value overnight. Many banks and businesses were ruined, and worldwide depression resulted.

Food distribution, Berlin 1931

US stopped lending money to Germany and demanded all loans be repaid.

German businesses:
• had to pay back loans
• received no more investment from the US
• had to pay increased taxes to government.

German government:
• couldn't borrow money from the US
• refused to print more money
• increased taxes
• made cuts in unemployment benefit
• government workers had wages cut and some lost their jobs.

German people
• Millions of workers and farm labourers lost their jobs.
• Young people were badly affected by job losses.
• With no work, and benefits slashed, families suffered terrible poverty.

Why the Depression increased support for extremist parties

• Democracy seemed to be failing as the moderate parties in the Reichstag failed to work together to solve the problems. The Weimar government was so weak, the Chancellor had to ask the president to pass emergency laws.

• Many working-class people turned to the extreme left-wing party, the Communists (KPD), who seemed to offer solutions to unemployment and falling wages.

• Many middle- and upper-class people turned to the extreme right-wing party, the Nazis, because they were afraid of the Communists gaining power and taking over their businesses.

• Germans from all sectors of society turned to the Nazis because they wanted a strong government who promised to restore law and order and workable economic policies.

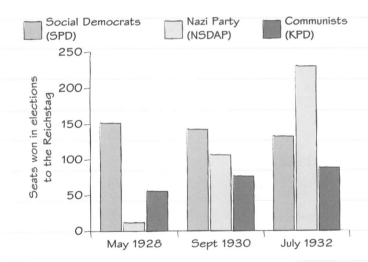

Social Democrats (SPD)   Nazi Party (NSDAP)   Communists (KPD)

Seats won in elections to the Reichstag

May 1928   Sept 1930   July 1932

The two most extreme parties in the Reichstag, the Nazis and the Communists, won support during the Depression at the expense of moderate parties such as the SPD.

To consider the appeal of Hitler and other reasons why support for the Nazis increased so spectacularly in this period, look at page 15.

Now try this

Explain **one** of the most important impacts of the Depression.

Hitler's appeal

Hitler was a major reason why the Nazi Party won far more votes in the 1930 and 1932 elections than in 1928. He took full advantage of the desperation people felt during the Depression. The **SA** also played an important role.

Reasons for Hitler's popularity

After the Munich Putsch and writing *Mein Kampf*, Hitler was fairly well known. His fame increased when he ran in the 1932 presidential election. He lost to Hindenburg but won many votes and many people were impressed by him.

> For a reminder about the Munich Putsch and *Mein Kampf*, look at page 10.

Hitler was portrayed as 'one of the people' – a worker and soldier – who therefore understood ordinary people's problems and what they wanted.

Hitler was an effective and rousing speaker; he travelled all over the country giving speeches in person or on the radio.

Hitler's speeches and propaganda were carefully designed to promise different things to different groups (wealthy and poor, rural and urban, young people and women). He therefore managed to gain wide support across society.

Hitler was a major feature of most Nazi election posters and pamphlets as he was seen as the main asset of the party. This poster from 1932 says 'Long live Germany!', linking Hitler with the nation.

Hitler came across as forceful and decisive, giving the impression he would be a strong leader for Germany. In the chaos caused by the Depression this was important to people.

Support from wealthy businessmen enabled the Nazis to pay for propaganda and for Hitler's travel, and to use new technologies such as the cinema and aeroplanes.

Factors that explain Hitler's appeal

- He kept his ideas vague and changed the message for different audiences, thereby appealing to a wide range of people.
- He constantly emphasised the failures of Weimar and his forceful style came across as the polar opposite of indecisive Weimar politicians.
- Gaining the support of some business leaders added to his appeal as well as helping finance his campaign.
- Propaganda was used very effectively.
- The SA played a major role, using fear and violence to stand up to Communists and sabotage opposition parties.

The role of the SA

The **Sturmabteilung** (Stormtroopers), or SA, were a paramilitary force. Formed in 1921 by Hitler, they were led by Ernst Röhm and wore brown uniforms. In 1930 they numbered about 400000, and grew to around 3 million by 1934. Many members of the SA were unemployed former soldiers. They played a major role in increasing support for the Nazis during the elections of 1930 and 1932 as they seemed to be able to control unrest on the streets by standing up to the Communists' paramilitary force. Their use of fear and violence to disrupt meetings and rallies, destroy publicity material, and beat up and intimidate opposition candidates effectively sabotaged opposition parties.

Now try this

> Use this page, and page 14, to answer this question.

Give **five** reasons why Hitler was able to gain so much support from the German people in the years 1928–32.

Hitler becomes Chancellor

Weimar parties lost electoral support in the elections between 1928 to 1932. This failure of Weimar democracy, together with the plotting of key figures – including President Hindenburg, Schleicher and Papen – led to Hitler's appointment as Chancellor in 1933.

Timeline

June 1928 Hindenburg appoints Hermann Müller, leader of the SDP, as Chancellor

March 1930 Grand Coalition government collapses as parties disagree on ways to tackle the Depression; Hindenburg appoints Heinrich Brüning, leader of the Centre Party, as Chancellor

1931/1932 The government does not have a Reichstag majority so cannot pass many laws – increasingly Brüning asks Hindenburg to pass laws by decree; between February and September, Reichstag doesn't meet

April 1932 Presidential election – Hindenburg is re-elected with 53% of the vote, but Adolf Hitler wins 36% and Ernst Thalmann (leader of KPD) wins 11%; Brüning bans the SA; he announces a plan to buy up land from landowners and use this to house the unemployed (both plans are unpopular with the Reichstag and Hindenburg)

June 1932 Hindenburg appoints Franz von Papen as Chancellor on the suggestion of Kurt von Schleicher; Papen is not a member of the Reichstag and heads a 'Cabinet of Barons', which features only two Reichstag members to govern Germany

September 1932 Reichstag passes a vote of no confidence in Papen's government; Papen calls another election

December 1932 Hindenburg appoints Schleicher Chancellor

May 1928 Reichstag elections – the moderate parties win the most votes

October 1929 Wall Street Crash

September 1930 Reichstag elections – major gains made by extreme parties

March 1932 Presidential election – no candidate wins 50% of the vote

May 1932 Brüning resigns

July 1932 Reichstag elections – the Nazis become the largest party but don't have a majority; Hindenburg refuses to make Hitler Chancellor; Papen continues as Chancellor, ruling through presidential decree rather than with the support of the Reichstag

November 1932 Reichstag elections – Nazis lose votes but is still the largest party; Hindenburg refuses to make Hitler Chancellor but sacks Papen on Schleicher's advice

January 1933 Schleicher has little support either inside or outside the Reichstag; Papen persuades Hindenburg to appoint Hitler as Chancellor and himself vice-Chancellor

The role of Papen

General Franz von Papen

- Undermined the Weimar Republic through ruling with Cabinet of Barons who, except for two, were not members of the Reichstag.
- Although he disliked Hitler, he agreed with many of his ideas and thought he would be able to control Hitler with Hindenburg's help.

The role of Hindenburg

Paul von Hindenburg

- Undermined the Weimar Republic by appointing chancellors who were not in the Reichstag, and was happy to rule by decree as never fully supported the Weimar Republic.
- Underestimated Hitler and thought he would be able to control him with the help of Papen.

Now try this

Give **two** examples of how Weimar democracy failed in the period 1930–32.

Removing opposition

Now the Nazis and Hitler were in power, they used the opportunity caused by the Reichstag fire to pass the Enabling Act (1933) and then removed the remaining political opposition to secure a dictatorship.

The Reichstag Fire

1 A lone Dutch communist was executed for starting the fire but Hitler seized the opportunity to accuse the Communist Party of a conspiracy against the government. Four thousand communists were arrested.

2 It gave Hitler an excuse to issue the emergency Decree for the Protection of People and the State, giving him powers to imprison political opponents and ban opposition newspapers.

3 He persuaded Hindenburg to call an election in March 1933 to secure more Nazi seats.

4 The Nazi Party managed to secure two-thirds of the seats by using the emergency powers to prevent the communists from taking up their 81 seats.

5 Hitler was now able to change the constitution.

The Reichstag fire of 27 February 1933. Marinus van der Lubbe was arrested and executed for starting the fire – some people believed the Nazis had started the fire deliberately.

The Enabling Act, 1933

Hitler proposed the Enabling Act in order to destroy the power of the Reichstag and give himself total power to make laws. It stated that:

☑ the Reich Cabinet could pass new laws

☑ the laws could overrule the constitution

☑ Hitler would propose the laws.

Result: Germany would no longer be a democracy.

Hitler expected resistance to the act and so used the SA to intimidate the opposition. The vote was won by the Nazis 444 to 94.

The elimination of political opposition and trade unions

Timeline

31 March 1933 Regional parliaments were closed down and reorganised with Nazi majorities (they were banned in January 1944)

May 1933 Offices and finance of other political parties were confiscated by the Nazis

22 June 1933 The SPD was banned as 'hostile to the nation and the state', then the Centre Party and German Nationalist Party dissolved themselves before they too could be banned

February/March 1933 The Communist Party was finished after the Reichstag fire; most communists who had not been arrested and put into concentration camps left the country

April 1933 Nazi opponents were rooted out from the civil service and the law

May 1933 Trade union offices were broken into, and officials were arrested and sent to concentration camps; then trade unions were banned – all workers belonged to the new German Labour Front

14 July 1933 The Law against the Formation of New Parties banned any political party except the Nazis

Now try this

Write a paragraph to explain how the Reichstag fire enabled the Nazis to increase their power in Germany.

Hitler becomes Führer

Having removed the threat of other political parties and trade unions, Hitler turned his attention to the SA. After this, President Hindenberg was the only person standing between him and total power.

The Night of the Long Knives

- Hitler decided he wanted to rid himself of the threat of Röhm and the SA. He did this by inviting Röhm and 100 SA leaders to a meeting in the town of Bad Wiessee on 30 June 1934. It was a ruse – when the leaders arrived they were arrested by the SS, taken to Munich and shot.

- After the arrests, Papen's staff were arrested and he was put under house arrest. Papen was no longer able to watch what Hitler was up to.

- Further killings occurred, including that of Schleicher.

It was thought that not many people fully realised how many people were being killed – many were relieved that the power of the SA had been reduced.

The SS was set up by Hitler in 1925 to act as his bodyguards. They were a select group run firstly by Schreck and then by Himmler. They appeared menacing in their black uniforms.

Why Röhm and the SA were removed

- Röhm led at least 3 million SA, which potentially made him a very serious rival, especially as he disagreed with some of Hitler's policies.

- Many important people in Germany, including Hindenburg, disapproved of the SA. Some of them were violent thugs who lacked any discipline.

- The German army only numbered about 100 000. Officers believed Röhm wanted to make the SA the new army. Hitler needed the army's allegiance.

- The other Nazi paramilitary force, the SS, was more disciplined. Its leader, Himmler, was closer to Hitler than Röhm; he wanted to reduce the size and influence of the SA to increase the power of the SS. Hitler agreed, partly because he was worried about the SA's reputation.

For a reminder about the SA, look at page 15.

SS troops guarding Hitler as he makes a speech, May 1934

The Sturmabteilung (SA)

Hitler becomes Führer

On 2 August 1934, just a few weeks after the Night of the Long Knives, President Hindenburg died. By this time, he was the only person preventing Hitler from having total power in Germany. Within hours of his death, a law concerning the Head of State merged the offices of Chancellor and President to create a new office of Führer. Hitler also announced that from now on the army would swear an oath of allegiance to him, not to Germany.

Führer means 'leader' and Hitler used propaganda to ensure that he looked all powerful. The 'Heil Hitler!' Nazi salute made people swear loyalty to him personally, and he was portrayed as having superhuman, heroic qualities.

After 2 August 1934, Hitler had complete control. Other political parties and opponents had gone, there was no longer a president and the armed forces were now under his command.

Now try this

Use the information on page 17, as well as this page, in your answer.

Construct a flow chart to explain the steps Hitler took to establish his dictatorship in 1933 and 1934.

Employment

In 1933 Germany was still suffering badly from the Depression, so the first priorities for the Nazis were to improve the economy and reduce unemployment.

Economic policies, 1933–36

Although the German economy had already started to grow before Hitler came to power, the Nazis did revive the economy. They:

- invested huge sums of money in public works programmes
- gave loans, subsidies and tax relief to businesses to increase production and take on more workers
- put controls on wages and prices to avoid hyperinflation
- controlled imports and made new trade agreements which increased trade and production in the New Plan of 1934.

To learn more about Nazi economic policies and rearmament, look at page 20.

National Labour Service (RAD)

- This was started by the Weimar government and continued under the Nazis.
- From July 1935, it was compulsory for all men aged 18–25 to serve for six months on this scheme.
- They worked on public works programmes or on farms.
- Many hated RAD. The pay was low, the hours long and the work boring.

Hjalmar Schact

President of the Reichsbank (1923–39), Schacht is recognised as a financial genius, credited with reviving the German economy. Hitler made him Minister for the Economy in 1934. He lost his job after a disagreement about rearmament in 1937.

Employment

Nazi economic policies and **rearmament** reduced unemployment. However, many people were taken out of the jobs market, which distorted the employment figures:

- many Jews were forced out of jobs

- many women were dismissed from or left their jobs

- unmarried men under 25 had to do National Labour Service for six months

- after 1935 more and more men over 18 were **conscripted** into the armed forces (they were required by law to join)

- opponents of the regime were sent to **concentration camps** (forced labour camps).

Building new schools and hospitals

Building 7000 km of **autobahns** (motorways)

Building and improving sports facilities (such as stadia for the 1936 Berlin Olympics)

Examples of public works programmes

Planting trees

Draining marshes to create more farmland

Building and improving public buildings, (such as the Chancellery in Berlin)

Building new houses

Laying new railway lines or extending existing ones

Several large projects were financed by the government to improve infrastructure, give private companies work and reduce unemployment.

Hitler making a start on the first autobahn in 1933

Now try this

Give **at least three** ways in which the Nazis reduced unemployment.

Nazi economic policies

From 1936, Nazi economic policies were geared towards preparing for war. **Rearmament** and **self-sufficiency** were the main aims. The economic policies had benefits and drawbacks for the people.

The Four-Year Plan, 1936–40

Hitler played a major role in devising this policy. Hermann Goering was made Minister for the Economy in 1937, so he was responsible for carrying out the plan. Its main aims were:

- rearmament to provide the weapons, vehicles and equipment for the rapidly expanding army, navy and airforce
- to make Germany self-sufficient in raw materials and food to try to avoid the problems of the First World War.

For more on the problems, see pages 6 and 8.

The plan was hugely expensive and only partially successful.

Self-sufficiency

- The policy of **autarky** (self-sufficiency) was a failure. In 1939 Germany was still dependent on imports for one-third of its raw materials.
- Farmers were given subsidies and cheap labour from RAD but food production grew only slightly.
- Campaigns to make Germans buy German goods met with partial success.
- Controls were put on imports but luxury imported goods actually increased.
- Scientists were funded to find substitutes for resources Germany did not have such as oil, rubber and cotton, but had little success.

Rearmament

German rearmament began in 1933 but was kept secret until 1935. It increased dramatically from 1936. By 1940 Germany had rearmed to an extent but hadn't met the Four-Year Plan targets.

- Some businesses benefitted from designing, providing materials and manufacturing arms.
- More jobs were created, and prisoners in labour and concentration camps were also used. However, by 1939 there were labour shortages.

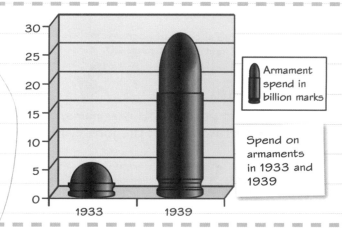

Armament spend in billion marks

Spend on armaments in 1933 and 1939

Nazi economic policies: pros

- 👍 Unemployment was reduced and most men were in work.
- 👍 Average weekly wages rose from 86 marks (1932) to 109 marks (1939) despite wage restrictions.
- 👍 Some businesses benefitted from increased investment and opportunities.
- 👍 Large businesses especially benefitted from the wage restrictions and loss of the trade unions.
- 👍 The Public Works Programmes provided better transport, services and homes.
- 👍 Some farmers benefitted from rising food prices, increased subsidies and cheaper labour.

Nazi economic policies: cons

- 👎 The cost of food rose – cancelling out wage increases.
- 👎 Working hours increased, especially after 1936.
- 👎 Some businesses resented the restrictions put upon them.
- 👎 The emphasis on using German goods meant that, in some cases, that available products were inferior.
- 👎 The Four-Year Plan put pressure on the economy and led to food and other shortages in the late 1930s.
- 👎 Some groups suffered; for example, Jewish businesses were boycotted and closed.

Now try this

Give **three** ways in which the Four-Year Plan can be seen as a) a success and b) a failure.

The impact of war

The German people were affected from the start of the Second World War in September 1939 but as the war progressed the impact on the economy and on German civilians increased.

The years 1939–42

- A **rationing** (fixed allowance) system for food was set up in August 1939, before the war began. Rationing for soap, clothing and fuel followed soon after.

- There were few shortages to begin with as food and goods were sent back to Germany from countries the army occupied. There was a thriving **black market** (illegal trade) for luxury goods for those that could afford to pay high prices. From late 1941 rationing was more severe as the army became bogged down in Russia.

- Foreign workers from occupied countries were sent to Germany to try to make up for **labour shortages.** Prisoners of war and inmates of concentration camps were also used as forced labour.

'Total War'

By 1941, the failures of the Four-Year Plan became more obvious as the German army suffered from shortages of weapons and equipment. Albert Speer became Armaments Minister in 1942 and made substantial changes that increased production. From 1943, Germany was on a 'Total War' footing where the whole economy was geared towards the war.

- Any businesses not involved in war work or food production were closed.

- Except for cinemas, which were used for propaganda films, places of entertainment were all closed.

- Some services such as the post were suspended.

All workers from the closed businesses and services were moved into war work. These changes did improve the supplies to the army.

Refugees

By July 1944 the German armies were in retreat from the Soviet Union's Red Army. Millions of refugees living in Poland, East Prussia and Czechoslovakia flooded into Germany ahead of the Russian advance. From January 1945, Russian troops entered Germany and millions more fled to western areas to escape. Cities already suffering from bombing and severe shortages of food and other essentials were therefore put under increasing pressure.

The impact of
war 1942–45

Bombing

From March 1942 to May 1945, German cities were repeatedly bombed by Britain and the US.

- Up to 500 000 people were killed and 750 000 wounded in bombing raids.

- Over a million homes were destroyed, leaving over 7 million homeless.

Extensive bombing damage

- Many Germans left the cities for the comparative safety of rural areas.

- Damage to supply lines and factories disrupted industrial production of goods, particularly of armaments.

- Thousands of businesses were seriously affected as property and goods were destroyed.

Rationing

Queues for food

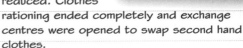
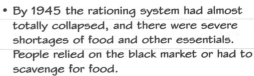

- From 1943 shortages of food and other goods increased, so rations were reduced. Clothes rationing ended completely and exchange centres were opened to swap second hand clothes.

- By 1945 the rationing system had almost totally collapsed, and there were severe shortages of food and other essentials. People relied on the black market or had to scavenge for food.

Labour shortages

- After January 1943, all men aged 16–65 and women aged 17–45 had to register for work. (Women were exempt if they were pregnant, had two or more young children or were farmers' wives.)

- Boys and girls from the Hitler Youth and League of German Maidens (BDM) helped with farm work.

- Forced labour increased dramatically to include Russian prisoners of war and people in labour and concentration camps.

Now try this

Explain **three** ways in which the Second World War had an impact on German people.

Impact on women

The Nazis introduced a range of policies directly aimed at women, which affected women's lives in lots of ways.

Reasons for policies

The Nazis had very traditional views about women, how they should behave and what they should look like. Their ideas about women directly influenced their policies. Women's main role was to breed and raise a 'master race' of Germans, which would make Germany bigger and stronger.

To have a natural appearance with long hair tied back and no make-up.

To be a non-drinker and non-smoker.

To wear traditional clothes.

To marry and have children.

To be fair haired and blue eyed (Aryan).

To believe in the Nazi ideas of Kinder, Küche, Kirche (children, kitchen, church).

The role of women in Nazi Germany

To be sturdily built (for child bearing).

To stay at home and not go to work or to university.

Nazi policies aimed at women

Policy	Practices	Impact on women
Women should not work, especially those who were married.	From 1933, women were banned from professional careers. **Propaganda** (information to spread ideas) was used to persuade women to stay at home and not 'take men's jobs'.	During 1933–36 the number of employed married women fell. However, after 1939 there was a shortage of workers as men left to fight the war. This meant women were encouraged back into work and the number of employed married women rose again.
Women should get married.	The Law for the Encouragement of Marriage (1933) initiated the use of vouchers (marriage loans) to newly married couples if the woman agreed to stop working.	The number of marriages did increase. However, it's not clear if this was due to Nazi policy or to other reasons such as a stronger economy.
Women should have at least four children.	Couples were let off one-quarter of their marriage loan repayments for each child they had. From 1936 women were given monthly payments to help with the cost of raising children. The German Women's Enterprise (DFW) gave women medals for having children.	The birth rate did increase but this may have been because the economy was improving rather than because of Nazi policies.
A woman's role should be to look after children and the home.	The DFW ran classes and radio programmes on home matters. Girls' education was tailored towards being a housewife. In 1937 grammar schools that prepared girls for university were banned.	The DFW had 6 million members, which suggests that many women welcomed Nazi policies. The number of women attending university dropped dramatically.

Now try this

Give **three** different examples of how the Nazis tried to 'persuade' women to have more children.

Young people and youth groups

The policies of the Nazis had a major impact on the lives of young people even outside school. Young people were encouraged to regard Hitler as a father figure and told that their first loyalty was to Nazi Germany, not to their families.

Reasons for policies

- To create proud Germans who supported a strong, independent Germany.

- To make sure the next generation would be loyal supporters of the Nazi Party and to believe in Nazi policies.

- To help children be strong and healthy so they would in turn produce many children of their own.

- To prepare girls for their future lives as wives, mothers and housekeepers.

- To prepare boys for their future lives as soldiers and workers.

Policies

- In 1933, the Nazis banned nearly all groups for young people except Nazi ones.

- Young people were increasingly under pressure to join the groups and many did so.

- Those who did not fit with Nazi racial ideas – Jews or disabled children, for example – were not allowed to join.

- From March 1939, it was compulsory for all young people to join Nazi youth groups.

Youth groups

There were four Nazi youth groups. Meetings and activities took place after school, at weekends and in the holidays.

Young German Folk (aged 10–14)   Young Girls (aged 10–14)   Hitler Youth (aged 14–18)   League of German Maidens (aged 14–18)

Examples of youth group activities

Boys	Both	Girls
Shooting	Hiking and camping	Cookery
Military drills	Learning about Hitler	Housework
Signalling	Learning about racial superiority	Needlework and craft
Military-style camps	Singing patriotic songs	Learning what to look for in a good husband
Helping the fire brigade during the war	Sport and competitions	Learning about babies and childcare
Formed military brigades to defend Berlin in 1945	Taking part in Nazi marches and rallies	
	Reporting people who made anti-Nazi comments	
	Collecting for Winterhilfe (a charity)	

Now try this

Look at the list of reasons for Nazi youth policies at the top of this page. Give an example of how youth groups helped to achieve each point.

Impact of education on the young

The Nazi education policy was designed to make German children loyal Nazis in preparation for their future roles in the Nazi state. Youth and education policies affected many aspects of young people's lives.

Nazi education policy

Schools	Teachers	Subjects	Propaganda
• Children had to attend state school until they were 14. • There were separate schools for girls and boys. • Optional schools after age 14: National Political Educational Institutes and Adolf Hitler Schools. • All schools followed a set curriculum – this was different for girls and boys.	• It was compulsory for teachers to be Nazi Party members. • Those who didn't teach Nazi ideas were dismissed. • Teachers' camps taught them how to use Nazi ideas in their teaching. • Nearly all teachers joined the Nazi Teachers' League. • Teachers were forced to attend courses to learn about Nazi ideas.	• 15% of time was spent on PE to ensure a healthy and strong population. • Girls were taught domestic skills; boys were taught science and military skills. • Both sexes were taught the traditional subjects: German, History, Geography and Maths. • New subjects: Race Studies and Nazi **Eugenics** were taught to both sexes.	• All lessons began and ended with the Hitler salute. • Nazi flags and posters decked classrooms. • From 1935 all textbooks had to be approved by the Nazi Party. • Traditional subjects were rewritten to glorify Germany, e.g. an emphasis on German writers and historical figures. • Racial ideas and anti-Semitism were taught within subjects.

Race Studies involved learning how to classify racial groups and about the superiority of the Aryan race. Eugenics is using controlled breeding to attempt to produce the 'perfect' human being.

It is difficult to measure the success of some of the policies – for example, how many children became totally loyal to the Nazi Party will never be known.

Many young people did join Nazi youth groups before they were forced to in 1939. However, there were very few extra-curricular options if you weren't in the Nazi Youth groups so this cannot be taken necessarily as evidence that they were very popular.

Generally – and there were exceptions – young Germans were more loyal and enthusiastic about Nazism than their parents. Many parents resented the time their children spent with youth groups. They believed their children were being undermined by Nazi teachings of loyalty to the state rather than the family.

Undoubtedly some young people found many of the activities offered by youth groups exciting and enjoyable, though the military discipline was often resented.

How successful were the Nazi youth and education policies?

Some young people opposed the Nazi youth groups and refused to go even when it was made compulsory. Some attended alternative groups who resisted and opposed Nazi ideas such as Swing Youth and the Edelweiss Pirates.

The activities of the youth groups and physical education at school did generally improve the fitness of young people.

Many Nazi ideas such as **anti-Semitism** do seem to have been accepted by many young people.

To learn more about these groups, turn to page 33.

Now try this

Explain why the Nazis made the education of boys and girls different.

Think about the aims of Nazi education as well as the content of the lessons.

Churches and religion

The Nazis wanted total loyalty to Hitler. The Churches and religion were a potential threat to Hitler and he therefore tried to control the Churches' influence.

Why were the Churches a threat to Hitler's ideas?

Nazi beliefs	Christian beliefs
Hitler as all-powerful leader	God as the ultimate authority
Aryan racial superiority	Everyone equal in the eyes of God
War, military discipline and violence important	Peace is what everyone should strive for
Dominance of the strong over the weak	The strong should look after the weak

The Catholic Church

The Nazis were particularly worried about the Catholic Church as Catholics were loyal to the Pope and had Catholic schools and youth organisations.

⬇

At first, Hitler tried to work with the Catholic Church. In July 1933, he reached a **concordat** (agreement) with the Pope that Catholics were free to worship and schools could continue as they were. However, the bishops had to swear loyalty to the Nazis and all clergy had to stay out of politics.

⬇

Hitler broke his promises when he banned Catholic youth organisations, closed Catholic schools that failed to teach the curriculum that other schools had to teach, and closed some churches and many monasteries.

⬇

In 1937, the Pope spoke out against Hitler in his statement known as 'With Burning Anxiety', which criticised Nazi policies. Some priests spoke out against the regime. They were harassed and/or sent to concentration camps.

The Protestant Churches

Many Protestants initially supported the Nazis because they feared communism. In the summer of 1933, the different Protestant churches within Germany were merged to form the **Reich Church**, led by Ludwig Müller, which:

- supported Nazi views and policies that excluded Old Testament teachings as they were Jewish
- dismissed any non-Aryan members
- sometimes displayed Nazi symbols and had some members who wore Nazi uniforms and called themselves German Christians.

However, not all Protestants accepted the Nazi state.

The **Confessional Church**, led by Martin Niemöller, was set up in 1934. This church:

- was in opposition to the Reich Church and many aspects of the Nazi regime
- taught only what was found in the Bible.

The Nazis tried to repress the Confessional Church. Some churches were closed, members were harassed and some pastors sent to concentration camps.

How far were churches under Nazi control?

- There were 6,000 Protestant churches in the Confessional Church, but only 2,000 in the Reich Church.
- Many opponents of the Nazis were religious.
- Most people who attended churches did little to oppose the Nazis, though it's difficult to assess whether this was because they supported the regime or were too frightened to oppose it.

SA troops outside a pro-Nazi church service, July 1933

Now try this

List **three** ways that the Churches co-operated with the Nazis, and **three** ways they resisted.

Aryan ideas

One of Hitler's main beliefs that was behind many Nazi policies was his idea of 'pure Germans', an 'Aryan' race he believed was superior to other people. Many people were excluded from this idea of racial perfection.

The perfect German 'Aryan'

Tall

Blue-eyed

Men: athletic and strong, for work or being a soldier

Women: athletic and strong for producing lots of children

Blond-haired

Aryans were those who the Nazis considered to be racially pure and perfect

Nazi racial hierarchy

Aryans
The 'master race'.

Other white western Europeans
Seen as fellow humans but lower than Aryans.

Eastern Europeans
Slavs – seen as 'sub-human'.

Black people and gypsies
Both seen as 'sub-human' and 'work-shy' (lazy).

Jews
Seen as lowest of 'sub-human' races and blamed for Germany's problems.

'Race farms' were set up where Aryan men and women met to have Aryan children. The SS were central to the Nazi master race, as they only recruited Aryans and were only allowed to marry Aryan women.

The German term for 'sub-humans' was **Untermenschen**. It was used by Nazis to describe Slavs, Roma, black people and Jews. Roma and Jews were seen as the worst of the *Untermenschen*. Hitler said they were not worthy of life.

Anti-Semitism

In Nazi ideology Jews were seen as a race rather than followers of a religion. Anti-Semitism was central to Nazi ideas. Jews were hated because:

* they were associated with communism
* they were often successful and people were jealous of them
* they were seen as alien because of their different religious practices, clothing and beliefs
* they were blamed for Germany's defeat in the First World War and the Treaty of Versailles (some of the Weimar politicians were Jewish).

There was a long history of anti-Semitism throughout Europe.

Other undesirables

As well as certain races not being included in the 'master race' there was no room in Nazi society for those they considered to be physically imperfect, not contributing to society, or behaving in ways they thought unacceptable. This wide range of people included:

* physically and mentally disabled people
* gay people
* tramps and beggars
* socialists
* trade unionists.

Karl Marx, the founder of communism, was from a Jewish family, as were some other communists in the USSR.

Now try this

Explain why the Nazis considered whole groups of people to be 'sub-human', and list **three** of the groups.

Racial policy and persecution

The Nazis introduced a wide range of racial policies. Many of these involved the persecution of Untermenschen and other people the Nazis thought undesirable. Generally, all persecution increased as time went on, particularly after the Second World War had begun.

Untermenschen

Racial policies affected everyone to differing degrees in Nazi Germany. The severity of the persecution depended on where they stood in the Nazi racial hierarchy.

- Aryans were banned from marrying or having sexual relations with any non-Aryan.

- Slavs were reminded continually that they didn't fit the Aryan ideal but there were fewer policies directed against them and they were persecuted less than other groups within Germany itself before 1939. However, attitudes towards Slavs certainly affected policy during the Second World War and Slav civilians across eastern Europe and the USSR were very badly treated by the invading Germany army.

- Mixed race children were sterilised.

- Roma people suffered from a range of policies which escalated in severity from 1933–45. However, treatment of Roma varied enormously depending on who and where they were.

- Seen as the 'lowest race', the worst policies and persecution were reserved for Jews.

Roma people

Timeline

1933–1935 Many were arrested and sent to concentration camps

1936 Some were sent to special camps

1938 All had to be registered, were examined and if they 'failed' the racial tests lost their citizenship and were banned from travelling

1939 They were told they would be deported out of Germany

1940–41 Some were deported to forced labour camps or Jewish ghettos in Poland. Some were later sent to Chelmno death camp

1942 Himmler ordered the deportation of all Roma from Germany. Most were sent to Auschwitz

1945 By the end of the war over 200 000 Roma had been killed – about 25% of the Roma population of Europe

To learn more about Jewish ghettos, Chelmno and Auschwitz, look at page 29.

Although conditions were terrible at Auschwitz, the Roma people were given certain privileges, such as being allowed to stay in family groups.

The Nuremberg Laws, 1935

The Reich Law on Citizenship

- Only those of German blood can be citizens.
- Non-Aryans will become subjects not citizens.
- Jews cannot vote, have a German passport or work for the government.
- People were defined as 'Jewish' if they had three or more Jewish grandparents.

The Reich Law for the Protection of German Blood and Honour

- No non-Aryan can marry a German citizen.
- No non-Aryan is allowed to have sexual relations with a German citizen.

Other 'undesirables'

- Gay men were sent to prison or concentration camps and subjected to medical experiments to correct their 'disorder' after laws against homosexuality were strengthened.

- Tramps and beggars were rounded up, put in concentration camps and made to do hard labour.

- The Law for the Prevention of Hereditarily Diseased Offspring (1933) led to the sterilisation of over 300 000 disabled people 1934–45.

- From 1939–45, severely disabled babies and children were killed by starvation or injection.

- From 1940–41, thousands of mentally ill and disabled adults were killed by gas in the **T4 Programme** until protests led by a Catholic bishop stopped this.

Now try this

The harsh treatment of the Roma people is a good example to use.

Describe how the Nazi policies on race became harsher as the 1930s wore on.

Jewish persecution

Persecution against Jews began with an attack on Jewish businesses and the removal of Jewish people from their jobs. **Kristallnacht** marked a turning point in the treatment of Jews.

Timeline

1934 Some Jews were banned from public places like parks and swimming pools; other councils painted park benches yellow specifically for use by Jewish people.

1936 Jews were banned or restricted from working as vets, accountants, teachers, dentists and nurses.

1938 Jews had to register their property. Jewish shops were set on fire or vandalised (Kristallnacht).

1933 The SA organised a one-day boycott of Jewish shops. They painted a yellow star on doors and discouraged people from going inside. Jewish actors and musicians were banned from performing. Jewish civil servants and teachers were sacked. Jews were no longer allowed to join the army or to inherit land. The SA also organised a one-day boycott of Jewish lawyers and doctors.

1935 The Nuremberg Laws, which placed further restrictions on Jewish life, were declared.

> For a reminder about the Nuremberg Laws, look at page 27.

1937 Jewish businesses were taken over by 'Aryans'. Jewish passports had to be stamped with a 'J'. 'Israel' or 'Sarah' had to added to Jewish names.

> For a reminder about 'Aryans', look at page 26.

1939 Jews were banned from owning businesses.

Kristallnacht (the Night of the Broken Glass), 1938

7 November
A 17-year-old Polish Jew entered the German embassy in Paris and shot a German.

↓

8 November
Goebbels used the event to stir up resentment against Jews by attacking homes and synagogues in Hanover.

↓

9 November
Goebbels and Hitler decided to increase the violence to a nationwide attack.

↓

9–10 November
Groups of uniformed and non-uniformed gangs ran amok amongst Jewish communities, destroying and burning homes, shops, businesses and synagogues.

100 Jews were killed. In addition, 814 shops, 171 homes and 191 synagogues were destroyed.

A Berlin shop destroyed during Kristallnacht, 1938

Consequences of Kristallnacht

Goebbels blamed the Jews for starting the trouble on Kristallnacht and ordered them to pay damages. Jews were fined 1 billion marks.

Now try this

Explain how Kristallnacht marked a turning point in the treatment of Jews in Nazi Germany.

The 'Final Solution'

During the Second World War, persecution of Jews reached levels not seen before. At some point during the summer of 1941, Nazi leaders decided on the 'Final Solution of the Jewish Question' – to exterminate Jews across all German territory in Europe.

Timeline

January 1939 The Reich Central Office for Jewish Emigration was set up to organise the deportation of Jews from Germany and Austria.

September 1939 The Second World War began.

October 1939 The first **ghettos** were built in Poland to separate Jews from the rest of the population. Over 1000 ghettos were eventually built, mostly in Poland and the Soviet Union.

January 1940 The T4 Euthanasia Programme began killing mentally ill and disabled adults in mobile gas units.

June 1941 Germany invaded the Soviet Union. SS killing squads known as **Einsatzgruppen** followed the German army and rounded up and killed all the Jews they could find.

December 1941 Chelmno death camp opened (for the first time Jews are killed by gas, in trucks).

January 1942 Leading Nazis met at the Wannsee Conference to decide the details of the 'Final Solution'.

March 1942 The first gas chambers were used to kill Jews at Belzec death camp.

As the German forces quickly conquered vast areas of Europe both in the west and east it brought many more Jews under Nazi control.

Ghettos were areas of a city enclosed by high walls with barbed wire on top. Guards shot anyone who tried to escape. Ghettos were very overcrowded and all goods entering them were severely restricted. Thousands died, mostly from starvation and disease.

Over 1 million Jews were killed by Einsatzgruppen. Victims were usually shot and buried in mass graves.

It is not clear exactly who took the decision to exterminate Jews some time in the summer of 1941, but many believe it was mainly Himmler's idea. Gas was chosen as the method because it had been successfully used in the T4 Programme.

All six death camps were in Poland. Hundreds of concentration camps were set up all over Germany from 1933 and in Nazi-occupied Europe after 1939.

Hundreds of thousands of Jews and other victims of the Nazis including Roma, homosexuals and political prisoners died in concentration camps 1933–45, from starvation, disease, overwork, shootings and beatings.

Most victims arrived at death camps by train from all over Nazi-occupied Europe, usually from concentration camps or ghettos. On arrival they were stripped, their hair shaved off and their possessions taken away. They were killed in gas chambers and buried in large pits or cremated in large ovens.

The 'Final Solution'

At Auschwitz, Jewish arrivals underwent a selection process where those found fit enough to work were sent to the concentration camp instead of the gas chambers.

At Madjanek and Auschwitz there were prison camps as well as the death camp so more survivors witnessed what was going on. The vast majority of people sent to the other four death camps were killed immediately.

How was persecution on this scale possible?

As well as the Nazi perpetrators themselves, many other Germans and people in Nazi-occupied Europe took part in some way (collaborators), such as those who planned the railway timetables. Millions of bystanders who knew at least something of what was going on did nothing to stop it, many because they were too afraid. There was resistance but it was fairly small-scale. Some helped to hide Jews and some Jews themselves resisted, such as those who took part in the Warsaw Ghetto Uprising. Resistors who were discovered were usually killed.

Now try this

Give **three** examples of how Nazi racial policy changed after the start of the Second World War.

Propaganda and censorship

Hitler wanted to use propaganda and **censorship** (government control over what people see and hear) to create a generation of people loyal to the Nazi regime and its values.

Joseph Goebbels

Played a central role as Nazi Minister of Enlightenment and Propaganda. He was a master at spreading Nazi ideas in a subtle as well as an unsubtle way. He essentially controlled newspapers, the radio, book publishing, film and the arts.

Methods of censorship

- ✓ Public burning of books by Jewish writers or others who disagreed with Nazi views.
- ✓ Radio producers, playwrights, filmmakers and newspapers were told what to say.
- ✓ Newspapers opposing the Nazis were closed.
- ✓ Only radios that couldn't receive foreign stations were made.

Methods of propaganda

Hitler featured in a lot of propaganda, either with a photograph or his name or title.

Posters showing Nazi beliefs were displayed everywhere.

Huge rallies and military parades were held, projecting a power and strength that would either make Germans proud of their country or fill them with terror, depending on their viewpoint.

The cinema showed propaganda films, but mainly entertainment films that had subtle Nazi messages.

Hitler made radio speeches which were played through loudspeakers in factories, cafés and on the streets. Entertainment programmes contained Nazi ideas and beliefs.

All sports teams had to give the Nazi salute and stadiums were covered with Nazi symbols. Sport was promoted as being central to Nazism. Victories for teams and individuals in sport were celebrated as victories for Nazism.

The Olympic games held in Berlin in 1936 promoted Nazi ideology. It was well organised and a grand spectacle so presented Nazi Germany in a good light.

Effects of propaganda

The Nazis' propaganda and censorship aims were largely met before 1943. They successfully controlled access to information, so that many Germans:

- only saw what the Nazis wanted them to see
- believed the messages
- supported most Nazi policies.

However, as the war began to go badly, people heard information from soldiers that contradicted the official news. When losing became inevitable and many German civilians experienced bombing and food shortages, most stopped believing the propaganda.

Now try this

List **at least five** methods the Nazis used to spread their ideas and beliefs.

Nazi culture

The Nazis had strong ideas about the cultural activities that should and should not be part of Germany. They particularly hated the modernist art associated with the Weimar period.

To remind yourself about Weimar culture, look at page 13.

Reich Chamber of Culture

- ✓ Set up in September 1993.
- ✓ Part of the Ministry of Propaganda and headed by Goebbels.
- ✓ Aimed to ensure that art, architecture, literature, music, theatre and film fitted with Nazi ideas.
- ✓ Banned things Nazis disagreed with and promoted things they really liked.

For a reminder about Goebbels' role, look at page 30.

The Chamber of Culture promoted paintings, sculptures, plays, films and books which:
- glorified war
- showed the superiority of Aryans
  For a reminder about Aryanism, look at page 26.
- showed the evil inferiority of Jews and Communists
- portrayed the ideal of motherhood and the family
- depicted Hitler as a great leader.

Architecture

- The Nazis liked public buildings to be very large and grand. They were often in the style of Ancient Rome and Greece with columns, pillars and steps.
- Buildings made of traditional materials such as stone and wood were preferred. Modern architecture was disapproved.
- Albert Speer was Hitler's favourite architect. He designed many major buildings such as the ground where rallies were held at Nuremberg.

Film

- Details of all planned films had to be approved by Goebbels, who also had to approve the final version before it could be shown.
- All cinemas had to show official Nazi newsreels before every film.
- The Nazi Party made its own films.

Look at pages 21 and 30 for more on film.

Music

- Music by those considered racially inferior was banned. Therefore music written by Jews was banned, as was jazz, which was associated with black musicians.
- Marching music and traditional classical music by composers such as Beethoven and Bach was preferred.
- Hitler loved the music of Richard Wagner because Wagner often composed music about traditional German heroes – so this music was especially promoted.

Culture in Nazi Germany

Literature

- Thousands of writers' works were banned either because they contained unacceptable ideas or because they were written by people, such as Jews, who were seen as racially inferior.
- Only new books approved by the Chamber of Culture could be published.
- Millions of banned books were burned on public bonfires.

Art

- Painters and sculptors were not allowed to produce, sell or teach art unless they were members of the Reich Chamber of Visual Arts.
- Artists were regularly visited by the Gestapo to check they were not breaking any rules.
- Unacceptable work such as impressionist art was removed from galleries.
- Large prizes were given for art competitions to encourage artists to produce work which the Nazis liked.

A painting on an approved topic – 'The Führer Speaks' by Paul Padua, 1939

Most artists either followed the rules or left Germany as their work could not be sold there. However, the Nazis were not completely successful in preventing people from accessing the art they considered unsuitable. For example, some people still managed to listen to jazz music and there were underground jazz clubs in some German cities.

Now try this

Give **three** examples of cultural works that were promoted by the Nazis.

The police state

A police state is where a government uses the police to control people's lives through **repression** (preventing someone from doing something through force or fear). While propaganda and culture were used to encourage loyalty to the Nazi regime, the **SS** and **Gestapo** were used for frightening people into behaving how the Nazis wanted them to and punishing those who did not.

Heinrich Himmler

Himmler, one of Hitler's closest colleagues, led the SS from 1929 and extended his power until he was in command of all police and security services. Himmler was a fervent supporter of Nazi racial policy. He also believed that he and the organisations he ran did not have to comply with the law if it was for the greater good of the Führer and Germany. After 1939, Himmler was put in charge of the occupied countries in the east and had overall control of racial policy.

The legal system

It was very difficult for anyone to get a fair trial in Nazi Germany.

☑ All judges had to belong to the National Socialist League for the Maintenance of the Law and had to favour the Nazi Party in their verdicts.

☑ Trial by jury was abolished and all verdicts decided by a judge.

☑ Cases of treason were tried in secret by specially selected judges.

The role of the SS

The SS played a major role in the police state.

- Members were trained to be highly disciplined and obedient so they would carry out any orders they received.
- They had unlimited powers to search property and arrest and imprison people without trial.
- Recruits had to be pure Aryans and were expected to marry Aryan wives to breed Aryan children.
- After 1936 the SS controlled the whole police system and ran the concentration camps.
- After 1940 a military wing, the Waffen SS was developed.
- During the Second World War, the SS was put in charge of the Einsatzgruppen and death camps.

The role of the Gestapo

The Gestapo was the secret police.

- Many members were professional police officers, not members of the Nazi Party.
- No uniforms made them hard to identify.
- Their main aim was to identify opponents.
- They spied on people using Party informants and the general population.
- They frequently used torture during questioning and sent many people to concentration camps.
- They were a small force (with never more than 50000 members, and far fewer before the war) but people were terrified.
- In 1936 they were led by Heydrich, under the control of Himmler and the SS.

Fear and intimidation: People believed there were Gestapo agents everywhere and were very worried about being sent to concentration camps. This meant that many people behaved as the Nazis wanted them to, as they were too afraid to do otherwise.

Stifling debate: People were careful about what they discussed, even with close family members, so there was very little questioning or debate about what the Nazis were doing, which restricted opposition and enabled the Nazis to carry on with their policies.

The impact on the German people

Encouraged spying: Although some informants were Nazi Party activists, most were just members of the public. They could be rewarded for information. Some people were loyal Nazi supporters but most informed on others because they were afraid or held personal grudges. So many people informed that it was impossible to investigate all allegations.

Now try this

Write a paragraph to explain how the Nazis used repression to control people.

Opposition, 1933–39

No one really knows how many German people opposed the Nazis but some individuals and groups openly resisted before the Second World War started.

Opposition and resistance

There were many ways people resisted Nazi rule, ranging from listening to banned music or telling anti-Nazi jokes to hiding Jews, speaking out against the regime or trying to kill Hitler. In general, though, there was very little open opposition to the regime because:

- people were too afraid of the SS, Gestapo and informers to risk it
- opposition groups were banned so it was difficult to join up with others who opposed the regime
- there was some genuine support for Hitler and his policies.

How were opponents dealt with up to 1939?

Opposition was dealt with effectively before the Second World War. Although people spoke out against the regime, the Nazis clamped down on them very quickly. Most were arrested and threatened into silence. Some were sent to concentration camps for 're-education'. Many opposition groups, such as the Edelweiss Pirates and Swing Youth, were cultural rather than political and had few members. The Nazis disapproved but did not consider them a serious threat, so few were seriously punished if caught.

For a reminder about opposition from some churches and individual Christians, look at page 25.

The Edelweiss Pirates

They were made up mainly of boys who copied an American style of clothing (checked shirts and white socks).

They were formed in the late 1930s, possibly as a consequence of Nazi policies enforcing Hitler Youth membership.

The Alpine flower, the edelweiss, was used as their symbol.

They were mainly based in working-class districts of large cities.

They sang 'Smash the Hitler Youth in twain, our song is freedom, love and life'.

The Nazis were not threatened by their activities.

By 1939 they had 2,000 members.

A group of Edelweiss Pirates in 1938.

They went on hikes and camping expeditions in the countryside to get away from Nazi restrictions.

They taunted the Hitler Youth.

They read and listened to banned music and literature and wrote anti-Nazi graffiti.

To remind yourself about Nazi youth groups, look at pages 23 and 24.

The Swing Youth

The Swing Youth also chose not to conform to Nazi ideas. They liked wearing American clothes, listening to American music and watching American films. They gathered to drink alcohol, smoke and dance. They organised illegal dances attended by thousands. Unlike the Edelweiss Pirates they were largely made up of children from wealthy families and could afford records and record players.

Now try this

In a short paragraph, explain why opposition groups such as the Edelweiss Pirates and Swing Youth were not treated harshly by the Nazis before 1939.

Opposition, 1939–45

After 1939, but particularly after 1942, more opposition groups emerged. Some of these groups existed before the Second World War, but now increased their opposition.

The White Rose Group

This group was set up at Munich University by Hans and Sophie Scholl and Kurt Huber.

- The white rose was a symbol of justice; the group was non-violent.
- Hans had seen the murder of Jews and other non-Aryans on the Eastern Front.
- The group let people know about the atrocities that were happening.
- It created and distributed leaflets opposing the Nazis and the war.
- All three leaders (plus other members) were eventually caught and executed.

Hans and Sophie Scholl (left), with Christoph Probst; members of the White Rose Group

Edelweiss Pirates and Swing Youth

During the war and especially from 1942 when the war began to go badly for Germany and people could see an end to the Nazi regime, resistance and opposition became more political and violent. More Swing Youth groups emerged in many German cities. The numbers of Edelweiss Pirates grew and they:

- spread Allied propaganda leaflets
- gave shelter to army deserters
- attacked members of the Hitler Youth and some Nazi officials – in 1944 they killed the head of the Cologne Gestapo.

Some Pirates were caught and hanged for their opposition.

Edelweiss Pirates being hanged in public for killing the head of the Gestapo in Cologne

The July Plot, 1944

Appalled by his experiences on the Eastern Front, Count Stauffenberg devised 'Operation Valkyrie'. This was a plot to assassinate Hitler, using a bomb in a briefcase.

At a military conference in East Prussia on 20 July 1944, Stauffenberg tried to blow up Hitler. The bomb exploded, but Hitler was only injured. Stauffenberg, along with 5746 others (including 19 generals and 26 colonels), was executed for his role. This highlights the deep opposition to Hitler from within the army towards the end of the war.

This seriously worried Nazi leaders so the army was brought under the control of the SS, which did reduce open opposition.

How effectively was opposition dealt with 1939–45?

- Any resistance or opposition to the Nazi regime during the war years was taken more seriously and therefore dealt with more harshly. For example, more members of Swing Youth who were caught listening to jazz and wearing inappropriate clothes were sent to concentration camps.
- The Nazis considered people who spoke out against the regime in war time as a serious threat and some were publically hanged or shot as a result.
- Opposition within the army was the first genuine threat to Nazi rule and again, those discovered plotting against the regime were killed as a warning to others.

Now try this

Choose **one** opposition group during the Second World War. Describe how this group opposed the Nazis and how effectively the Nazis dealt with this group.

Exam overview

This page introduces you to the main features and requirements of the Paper 1 Section A exam paper for Germany, 1890–1945: Democracy and dictatorship.

About Paper 1

- Paper 1 is for your period study and your wider world depth study.
- Section A of the paper will be on your period study, which is Germany, 1890–1945: Democracy and dictatorship.
- You must answer **all** questions in Section A.
- You will receive two documents: a question paper, which will **contain the questions and interpretations,** and an answer booklet.

> The Paper 1 exam lasts for 1 hour 45 minutes (105 minutes). There are 84 marks in total: **40 marks for Section A**; 40 marks, plus 4 marks for spelling, punctuation and grammar, for Section B. You should spend approximately 50 minutes on Section A and 50 minutes on Section B with 5 minutes to check your answers.

> Here we are focusing on Section A and your period study. However, the same exam paper will also include Section B, where you will answer questions about your wider world depth study.

The questions

The questions for Paper 1 Section A will always follow this pattern:

> You can see examples of all six questions on pages 38–43, and in the practice questions on pages 44–53.

Question 1

How does **Interpretation B** differ from **Interpretation A** about … ?

Explain your answer using **Interpretations A** and **B**.

(4 marks)

> Question 1 targets AO4. AO4 is about analysing, evaluating and making substantiated judgements. Spend about 5 minutes on this question, which is about the ways in which the interpretations differ.

Question 2

Why might the authors of **Interpretations A** and **B** have a different interpretation about …?

Explain your answer using **Interpretations A** and **B** and your contextual knowledge. **(4 marks)**

> Question 2 also targets AO4. Spend about 5 minutes on this question, which is about **suggesting and explaining why** the interpretations differ.

Question 3

Which interpretation do you find more convincing about …?

Explain your answer using **Interpretations A** and **B** and your contextual knowledge. **(8 marks)**

> Question 3 also targets AO4. You should spend approximately 10 minutes on this question, which is about **evaluating** the interpretations.

> Question 4 targets AO1. AO1 is about showing your knowledge and understanding of the key features and characteristics of the topic. Spend about 5 minutes on this question.

Question 4

Describe two … **(4 marks)**

Question 5

In what ways …?

Explain your answer. **(8 marks)**

> Question 5 targets both AO1 and AO2. AO2 is about explaining and analysing historical events using historical concepts, such as causation, consequence, change, continuity, similarity and difference. Spend about 10 minutes on this question, which focuses on **change**: explaining how a group or development was affected by something.

Question 6

Which of the following was the more important reason why …?

(Two bullet points)

Explain your answer with reference to both bullet points. **(12 marks)**

> Question 6 also targets both AO1 and AO2. Spend about 15 minutes on this question, which is about making a judgement and focuses on **causation, consequence, change and/or continuity**.

Interpretation skills

This exam asks you to analyse, evaluate and make judgements about interpretations.

What are interpretations?

For the first three questions in the exam paper you will be asked to study **interpretations** of a particular enquiry or event from two different people. Interpretations are compiled after the time period or event. Interpretations can be accounts of events written by people who were there or written by historians. They might also be images, such as reconstructive drawings or diagrams of events. All interpretations will contain people's views and opinions.

As well as analysing interpretations, you will need to evaluate them and make judgements about them. In all cases, you need to keep the **historical context** in mind.

Analysing interpretations

When analysing interpretations you need to try and work out the **message** of the interpretation. Do this separately for each interpretation and then compare them. You then need to think about the following for the exam questions:

- **how** they differ (question 1)
- **why** they differ (question 2)
- which interpretation is **more convincing** (question 3).

Look at each interpretation carefully. Underline information or annotate the interpretation with your ideas to help you identify key points that you can use in your answer.

Contextual knowledge

Questions 2 and 3 will both ask you to explain your answer using the interpretations and your **contextual knowledge**. This means that you need to think about what you know about the event or development and how the interpretations fit with what you know. Only use knowledge that's relevant to the topic in the question and is linked to what is discussed in the interpretation itself.

As you consider each interpretation, ask yourself: What do I know about these events/developments? How is this reflected in the interpretation? How is this linked to the focus of the question?

Provenance

Before both interpretations in the exam paper you will be given several lines of **provenance**. This will vary for each but is likely to include some details about the author and their work or experiences, and when their work was published. This information is as important as the interpretation itself as it will help you establish the **purpose** of the interpretation, which will help you in questions 2 and 3 in particular.

Provenance means where something comes from – where it started or came into existence.

Hints and tips for analysing and evaluating interpretations

How complete?	How objective?	What is the chosen emphasis?
The interpretations can be different because they are concerned with finding out about different aspects of the enquiry and may cover different ground. Sometimes, historians set out to look at one aspect specifically, whereas others may want to look at related issues in a broader sense.	Historians can hold different views because they come from a particular school of thought. Therefore, their questions and answers are shaped by their wider views of society and how it works and has worked in the past. This can have an important impact on the judgements and opinions they hold about historical matters.	Sometimes, historians use the same sources but reach different views because they place a different level of importance on the same evidence. They may have access to the same material sources as each other, but will draw different conclusions about the significance of that evidence.

Interpretations A and B

These interpretations are referred to in the worked examples on pages 38–40.

SECTION A

Germany, 1890–1945: Democracy and dictatorship

Read **Interpretations A** and **B** and answer questions 1, 2 and 3 on pages 38, 39 and 40.

Interpretation A   Jacques Delarue, in his book *History of the Gestapo*, published in 1964. Jacques Delarue was a member of the French Resistance who opposed the Nazis after the invasion of France during the Second World War. In researching evidence for this book, Delarue interviewed former agents and others who worked for the Gestapo.

For each interpretation you will be given short details on the work the interpretation comes from. In this case, the author, title of the book and when it was published.

You will be given a few lines of information about the author and/or the interpretation. In this case you are told that the author was a member of the French resistance and that he interviewed people who worked for the Gestapo as evidence for his book.

> Never before, in no other land and at no time had an organisation attained such a comprehensive penetration of society, possessed such power and reach such a degree of ... terror and horror, as well as ... effectiveness. The Gestapo spotted or overheard every German's slightest movement.

Interpretation B   Laurence Rees in his book, *The Nazis: A Warning from History*, published in 2001.
Laurence Rees is a British historian. This book was based on his TV series of the same title was made up of film footage and interviews with a variety of people who lived through Nazi rule including Nazi Party members, opponents of the Nazis and ordinary Germans.

For each interpretation, underline or highlight any important words or phrases and annotate them.

> Like all modern policing systems, the Gestapo was only as good or bad as the cooperation it received – and the files reveal that it received a high level of cooperation. Only around 10% of political crimes committed ... were actually discovered by the Gestapo; another 10% were passed on to the Gestapo by the regular police or the Nazi Party. Around 80% was discovered by ordinary citizens who turned the information over ... Most of this unpaid cooperation came from people who were not members of the Nazi Party – they were 'ordinary' citizens.

It's a good idea to compare and contrast the provenance of the two interpretations. Why might the authors have a different view? Are they looking at different things? At different times? In different ways?

Your annotations within the interpretation could also include any points that contrast with the other interpretation.

Question 1: Explaining how interpretations differ

Question 1 on your exam paper will ask you to identify differences in two interpretations: 'What is the main difference between the views ...'. There are 4 marks available for this question.

Worked example

Read Interpretations A and B on page 37.

How does **Interpretation B** differ from **Interpretation A** about the German public's support for the Nazis?

Explain your answer, using **Interpretations A** and **B**.   **(4 marks)**

Remember to include points from **both** interpretations. It's important to refer directly to the interpretation and include short quotations to support what you say.

Links You can revise methods of Nazi control and public support for the Nazis on pages 30–34.

How interpretations differ

In a question that asks **how** one interpretation differs from another, you need to analyse both interpretations and explain how they are different. Look for the important or key differences, not just surface details. A fundamental difference might be that they believe different factors are more important for explaining why something happened. A surface detail would just repeat content from two interpretations without explaining how they are different. You don't need to explain why they are different, as you will do this in question 2.

Sample answer

These interpretations are different because the first one says that the Gestapo heard everything, whereas the second historian says that some crimes were reported to the regular police, not the actual Gestapo.

 This answer focuses on a difference in surface details. Instead, you need to make sure you look for key, underlying differences in the interpretations.

Improved answer

In Interpretation A, Delarue argues that the Gestapo achieved 'comprehensive penetration' of German society. Therefore, the attitudes of the German public were fully controlled by the Gestapo. He claims the use of 'terror and horror' was successful in making sure that the public believed the Gestapo was all-knowing and 'overheard' all activities or even the smallest action. This differs from Interpretation B, where Rees states that the Gestapo's work in controlling people's attitudes was based more on a public willingness to cooperate with them, rather than due to terror. He backs this up by saying that 80% of political crimes investigated by the Gestapo were as a result of 'ordinary citizens', rather than Nazi party members denouncing people and reporting their 'suspicions' to the Gestapo.

Use short quotations to support your analysis.

 Make sure you focus on the key point of difference, rather than on more minor differences. Here the student does this well by picking out that Interpretation A claims the Gestapo were successful due to 'terror and horror' whereas Interpretation B claims they were successful due to public cooperation.

 You need to identify and explain a key difference, and support it with detailed points from both interpretations.

Think about the specific language you use in your answer, such as: 'argues', 'claims', 'states' and 'backs this up'. These phrases help you to produce a better answer because they help show you are analysing another person's judgement or opinion about something.

Question 2: Explaining why interpretations differ

Question 2 on your exam paper will ask you to explain why two interpretations give different views. There are 4 marks available for this question.

Worked example

Why might the authors of **Interpretations A** and **B** on page 37 have a different interpretation about the German public's support for the Nazis?

Explain your answer using **Interpretations A** and **B** and your contextual knowledge.

(4 marks)

Sample answer

One reason why Interpretations A and B have a different interpretation about the German public's support for the Nazis is because the authors have different focuses.

Delarue's specific focus for his research was on the 'history of the Gestapo'. Therefore, his concern was to explain the role of the Gestapo and terror organisations in Germany, rather than asking wider questions about support and cooperation from the German people. Much of the evidence he used to come up with his interpretation was based on interviews with Gestapo agents and others who worked for the Gestapo. They would probably have believed their work was extremely effective.

In contrast, Rees' focus was much wider and included assessing the extent of support given to the Nazi regime by the German public. His evidence was based on a wider variety of sources, including the thoughts of ordinary Germans. Therefore, as he consulted ordinary 'citizens', he discovered that many Germans willingly gave information to the Gestapo, which suggests they supported the Nazi regime at least to some extent rather than being too terrified to resist.

'Why' questions

In a question that asks you why authors have different interpretations, you need to offer and explain an idea about **why** there are differences. You need to show you understand that historical interpretations are judgements and opinions based on evidence, and that, as such, different views can exist.

 Links You can revise methods of Nazi control and public support for the Nazis on pages 30–34.

Remember: you **must** include your own contextual knowledge in your answer.

Starting your answer with a basic explanation of the differences – in this case, the different focus taken by each historian – is a good idea. Then you should go on to to give a deeper explanation.

You must always read the provenance of the interpretations carefully, as this student obviously has. It will give you important clues about the author's focus and the evidence used.

You could try to take into account the **context** of why the interpretations were written, explaining why there are differences.

As the student has done here, you must try to make the explanation as clear as possible and you must refer to **both** interpretations.

Question 3: Evaluating interpretations

Question 3 on your exam paper will ask you to evaluate two interpretations by asking which interpretation you find more convincing. There are 8 marks available for this question.

Worked example

Which interpretation do you find more convincing about the German public's support for the Nazis?

Explain your answer using **Interpretations A** and **B** on page 37 and your contextual knowledge.

(8 marks)

Sample extract

I find Interpretation A more convincing as I don't agree with the interpretation that there was a lot of support for the Nazis from ordinary Germans. They had to rely on concentration camps to get rid of opposition. They used terror and propaganda to control people. The public didn't really support the Nazis fully because there was opposition like the Edelweiss Pirates, so not everyone thought they should help them.

Which is more convincing?

You must:

- ✓ explore different views on the debate
- ✓ reach a clear **judgement** yourself
- ✓ give detailed knowledge of the **context** and wider issues
- ✓ use **both** interpretations – don't just rely on one.

🔗 **Links** You can revise methods of Nazi control and public support for the Nazis on pages 30–34.

Remember: you **must** include your own contextual knowledge in your answer.

Give your opinion clearly, as this student has done.

Always support the points you make with evidence from the interpretation and your own knowledge – the student doesn't do this here.

This student attempts to develop a line of argument, but it is not well chosen because the Edelweiss Pirates were a small group and not typical of Germany as a whole.

Improved extract

Delarue's claim that the Gestapo 'spotted or overheard every German's slightest movement' is an exaggeration as this cannot possibly have been the case throughout all of Germany with such a small organisation. However, I agree with Delarue that the Nazi regime maintained control of people through 'terror and horror'. While Rees provides evidence that 80% of ordinary Germans willingly gave the Gestapo information, cooperation with the Gestapo could itself be evidence that the public were fearful of not appearing to support the regime and felt coerced to 'name names'.

Active participation in the regime was demanded from the Nazi state and Nazi organisations were compulsory in all aspects of life, from the DAF, for workers, to the Hitler youth, for young men. Therefore, giving information to the Gestapo can be seen in this light. Although some people undoubtedly did support the Nazis, many people were terrified of the Gestapo and being sent to a concentration camp, and did whatever they could to avoid this happening.

You could highlight key points in the interpretations themselves to help you focus on the precise arguments that you need to evaluate in order to make your judgement.

This answer engages directly with both Delarue's and Rees' claims, and challenges both of them.

You need to put both interpretations into **context** as the student has done here by bringing in their own knowledge of the Gestapo and other methods of Nazi control.

Question 4: Describing features or characteristics

Question 4 on your exam paper will ask you to describe two features or characteristics of Germany 1890–1945. There are 4 marks available for this question.

Worked example

Describe two problems faced by the German people in 1918. **(4 marks)**

Sample answer

By 1918, army leaders were really running Germany and the Kaiser had been sidelined. It became increasingly obvious that Germany was going to lose the war so more and more soldiers started deserting the army. Sailors in the navy then mutinied and refused to obey orders. There was a lot of war weariness as thousands of men had been killed and thousands more injured. There were also serious shortages of food, medical supplies and raw materials so German civilians were suffering badly.

Improved answer

By 1918 there were serious shortages of food in Germany because the British Royal Navy stopped supplies reaching Germany by sea. Many people were malnourished and some died from starvation. Many survived on only turnips and bread.

By 1918 many German soldiers had been killed and many more injured leaving families without husbands, brothers and fathers. This meant many Germans were grieving but also meant many were worried about money because they would have to survive on war pensions from the government.

What does 'describe' mean?

Describe means give an account of the main characteristics of something. You should develop your description with relevant details to show that you understand them. However, you do not need to include reasons or justifications.

 Links You can revise the situation in 1918 on pages 6 and 7.

 Make sure you only give two problems and that you describe each one with some detail. This answer lists over five problems but gives little detail.

 Read the question carefully. This question asks for problems faced by the 'German people', so the information about army leaders and the Kaiser is irrelevant.

 It's a good idea to present your two problems in separate paragraphs as the student has done here. This shows clearly that you have identified two different problems.

 You need to give **supporting details** for each problem, as the student has done here.

Question 5: Explaining change

Question 5 on your exam paper will ask you to explain how a group or development was affected by something. There are 8 marks available for this question.

Worked example

In what ways were the lives of young people affected by Nazi policies?
Explain your answer.   **(8 marks)**

Sample extract

Shortly after the Nazis came to power in 1933, they banned many groups for young people and encouraged and pressurised young people into joining Nazi groups. There were four Nazi youth groups: Young German Folk for boys aged 10–14; Young Girls for girls aged 10–14; Hitler Youth for boys aged 14–18; and the League of German Maidens for girls aged 14–18. Many young Germans joined these groups, which met after school, at weekends and in the school holidays. Many of the activities of these groups were different from what young people would have experienced before. For both boys and girls there was an emphasis on health and exercise and learning about Nazi ideology. Girls were taught about looking after children and the home while boys were taught military skills such as shooting and signalling. Some young people may have done these things before but for most it would have been new. It also meant that many young people spent little time with their parents, which would have been unusual before 1933.

The point of the Nazi youth groups was to prepare children for their future roles in the Nazi state – boys as soldiers and workers, and girls as housewives and mothers – and to try to ensure that young people would be loyal supporters of Nazi policies.

There were a few young people who refused to join Nazi youth groups at all, even after they were made compulsory in 1939. Some joined alternative groups such as the Edelweiss Pirates or Swing Youth. For those few who didn't join Nazi groups their lives would have changed because they may have had to be secretive about the groups they did join.

Explaining 'in what ways'

This question requires you to describe and explain how and why a group or development **changed**. There will always be a number of different ways in which change happened. The best answers will also show that change was not the same for everyone or everything.

 Links You can revise Nazi policies on young people and education on pages 23–24.

 Give an example of **change**. This answer gives the example of how young people were encouraged to join Nazi youth groups. Support your example with **details**. This student gives details of each group along with examples of what young people did at these groups.

 It's a good idea to show how something was different from before. For example, here the student explains that many activities of the youth groups would have been unusual for children before the Nazis came to power.

 Try to explain the **reasons** for the changes that took place. In this case, the student points out that youth groups were trying to prepare young people for their future roles as the Nazis saw them, as well as trying to ensure loyalty to the regime.

 The best answers will show that not all people in the group behaved in the same way. This student describes how not all young people joined Nazi youth groups.

Although it isn't included in this extract, you should also describe changes in education and school life in an answer to this question, as the focus is on how the lives of young people were affected generally.

Question 6: Making a judgement

Question 6 on your exam paper will identify two reasons for you and ask you to analyse them. You will need to decide which was the more important reason why something did or did not happen. There are 12 marks available for this question.

Worked example

Which of the following was the more important reason for the growth in support for the Nazis between 1928 and 1932?

• The impact of the Depression
• The appeal of Hitler

Explain your answer with reference to both bullet points.

(12 marks)

Sample extract

Both the impact of the Depression and the appeal of Hitler were important reasons for the growth of support for the Nazis and both were connected to each other as Hitler used the impact of the Depression very effectively to rouse support for the Nazis. However, I think the impact of the Depression was the more important reason.

Hitler was an important factor because many people chose to vote for the Nazis in the Reichstag elections and for Hitler in the presidential elections because of Hitler's appeal. He was an excellent speaker and travelled all over the country giving rousing speeches in person and on the radio. He came across as 'one of the people' who understood their troubles and what they wanted. Perhaps most importantly however, he came across as a very strong and decisive leader, which was very appealing to many people when the Weimar government seemed to be indecisive and ineffective.

However, a major reason why Hitler was so appealing was due to the impact of the Depression on Germany. Without this it is very doubtful the Nazis would have attracted so much support. The Wall Street Crash in the USA in October 1929 led to worldwide economic depression. Germany was particularly badly affected because it had borrowed so much money from the USA in the years before 1929. The Depression meant not only that the US investment stopped but that Germany had to pay back the loans to the USA. Many banks and businesses were ruined meaning that millions of workers lost their jobs. The government increased taxes to try and pay back the loans and also cut unemployment benefit which meant many Germans were in a desperate situation and opposition to the Weimar government grew ...

The balance of Assessment Objectives

Question 6 is an essay question worth 12 marks in total. Of this, 6 marks are for AO1 and 6 marks are for AO2. Therefore you need to combine information and understanding (AO1) equally with analysis and explanation (AO2) for the best results. You also need to reach a judgement and follow a sustained line of reasoning that is coherent, relevant, substantiated and logically structured.

🔗 **Links** You can revise the growth of Nazis support on pages 14–15.

Begin your answer with a strong opening paragraph. This should lay out **your opinions** of the reasons given in the question and, most importantly, come to a **judgement** about which reason was more important.

You **must** explain **both** reasons given in the bullet points giving detailed information on what happened and why.

Only focus on the reasons given in the bullet points in the question, as the student has done here. You don't need to include any other reasons in your answer.

Make sure you show how the reasons are **connected** – here, the student points out that Hitler was appealing **because** of the impact of the Depression.

This is an extract from a student's answer. In a full answer, you would need to go on to explain why many people turned to the Nazis because of the Depression.

Practice

You will need to refer to the interpretations below in your answers to questions 1, 2 and 3 on pages 45–47.

SECTION A

Germany, 1890–1945: Democracy and dictatorship

Answer **all six questions** on pages 45 to 52.

Read **Interpretations A** and **B** below and answer questions **1, 2** and **3** on pages 45–47.

Interpretation A   Richard J Evans in his book *The Coming of the Third Reich*, published in 2004.
Richard Evans is a British historian who specialises in German history. In this book he examines Germany from 1871 to 1933 describing the origins of Nazi Germany.

> Nazi propaganda … skilfully targeted specific groups in the German electorate … providing topics for particular venues and picking the speaker to fit the occasion. The … Party recognized the growing divisions of German society into competing interest groups in the course of the Depression and tailored their message to their particular constituency. The Nazis adapted ... a whole range of posters and leaflets designed to win over different parts of the electorate.

Interpretation B   Ian Kershaw in his article 'The Hitler Myth', published in *History Today* Volume 35 Issue 11, November 1985.
Ian Kershaw is a British historian who has written many books on Nazi Germany and the Second World War. He is regarded as an expert on Hitler and has written several biographies on him.

> … more and more Germans saw in Nazism – symbolised by its leader – the only hope for a way out of gathering crisis. Those now surging to join the Nazi party were often already willing victims of the 'Hitler Myth'. Even for the vast majority of the German people who did not share such sentiments, there was the growing feeling … that Hitler was not just another politician, that he was a party leader extraordinary, a man towards whom one could not remain neutral.

Practice

Put your skills and knowledge into practice with the following question. You will need to refer to Interpretations A and B on page 44 in your answer.

1 How does **Interpretation B** differ from **Interpretation A** about Nazi tactics and support in the early 1930s?

Explain your answer, using **Interpretations A** and **B**.

(4 marks)

Guided .Interpretations .A .and .B .both .discuss .Nazi .tactics...
.and .support .but .offer .different .views.............................

....
....
....
....
....
....
....
....
....
....
....
....
....
....
....

You have 1 hour 45 minutes for the **whole** of Paper 1, which means you have 50 minutes for Section A. You should use the time carefully to answer all the questions fully. In the exam, remember to leave 5 minutes or so to check your work when you've finished both Sections A and B.

 Links You can revise Nazi support and tactics in the early 1930s on page 15.

You can revise how to evaluate interpretations on page 36.

Spend about 5 minutes on this answer. You need to identify the **key difference**, rather than just surface differences.

Make sure you refer to the content of **both** interpretations.

Remember to use specific words and phrases in your answer such as: 'argues', 'claims', 'states' and 'backs this up'. These help to show you are analysing another person's judgement or opinion.

It is a good idea to use short **quotations** from the interpretations to support your answer.

Practice

Put your skills and knowledge into practice with the following question. You will need to refer to Interpretations A and B on page 44 in your answer.

2   Why might the authors of **Interpretations A** and **B** have a different interpretation about Nazi tactics and support in the early 1930s?

Explain your answer using **Interpretations A** and **B** and your contextual knowledge.

(4 marks)

....

....

....

....

....

....

....

....

....

....

....

....

....

....

....

....

....

....

....

You should spend about 5 minutes on this answer.

You can revise how to evaluate interpretations on page 36.

Links You can revise Nazi support and tactics in the early 1930s on page 15.

Remember that the **provenance** information given before each interpretation will help you with this question.

It is essential to use your **own contextual knowledge** in answering this question.

A good way of answering this specific question is to think about the focus of each historian. Kershaw's focus is specifically on Hitler, whereas Evans is looking at wider issues.

Make sure you refer to **both** the interpretations to support your answer.

Practice

Put your skills and knowledge into practice with the following question. You will need to refer to Interpretations A and B on page 44 in your answer.

You should spend about 10 minutes on this question.

3 Which interpretation do you find more convincing about Nazi tactics and support in the early 1930s?

Explain your answer using **Interpretations A** and **B** and your contextual knowledge.

(8 marks)

You can revise how to analyse interpretations on page 36.

Guided   I find Interpretation .... more convincing because ....

Say which interpretation you find more convincing in the opening sentence: A or B.

....

....

....

🔗 **Links**   You can revise Nazi support and tactics in the early 1930s on page 15.

....

....

....

Start with a clear **judgement** about which interpretation you think is more convincing. You could also include reasons why the other interpretation is less convincing at this stage.

....

....

....

It's essential to refer to **both** interpretations throughout your answer.

....

....

....

....

....

....

Remember to include your own knowledge of the **context** – about the appeal of Hitler and Nazi use of propaganda and targeting specific groups in winning support for the Nazis.

....

....

....

....

....

....

You should build an argument throughout your answer, giving a number of reasons why one interpretation is more convincing and the other one less convincing.

....

Practice

Use this page to continue your answer to question 3.

....

....

....

....

....

....

....

....

....

....

....

....

....

It doesn't really matter which interpretation you find more convincing. There isn't a 'correct' answer, just your own opinion. What's important is to explain **why** you think that particular interpretation is more convincing and support your reasons with **evidence** from your contextual knowledge.

Practice

Put your skills and knowledge into practice with the following question.

4 Describe two problems faced by the German people in 1945.

(4 marks)

....

....

....

....

....

....

....

....

....

....

....

....

....

....

....

....

....

....

....

You should spend about 5 minutes on this question.

Links You can revise problems faced by the German people in 1945 on page 21.

Only describe **two** problems. You won't receive any credit for describing more than two and will waste valuable time if you do.

Write a separate paragraph for each of your two problems. This will show you have identified two different problems.

You need to include some **details** for each problem. This will show that you understand **how** it was a problem.

Problems could include rationing and food shortages; conscription into the work force; impact of bombing; impact of refugees.

Practice

Put your skills and knowledge into practice with the following question.

5 In what ways were the lives of people in Germany affected by the Second World War?

Explain your answer.

(8 marks)

....

....

....

....

....

....

....

....

....

....

....

....

....

....

....

....

....

....

....

....

....

....

....

You should spend about 10 minutes on this question.

Links You can revise the impact of the Second World War on page 21.

You need to identify the **changes** in people's lives. Remember to include a number of different ways in which people's lives were affected.

Each example of change you describe must be supported with **detail**.

Remember to explain how the change was **different** from before. For example, before 1939 women were discouraged from working as the Nazis thought they should focus on looking after children and the home. However, during the war women were conscripted into work, so more women became employed.

You could include examples from a variety of different things such as rationing, work and the impact of Allied bombing.

Practice

Use this page to continue your answer to question 5.

....

....

....

....

....

....

....

....

....

....

....

....

> For each change you describe, try to explain the **reason** why this change happened. For example, more women were conscripted into work to deal with labour shortages because many men had been conscripted into the armed forces.

Practice

Put your skills and knowledge into practice with the following question.

6 Which of the following was the more important reason for the establishment of the Nazi dictatorship in the years 1933 to 1934?

- The Enabling Act, 1933
- The elimination of political opposition

Explain your answer with reference to both bullet points.

(12 marks)

You should spend about 15 minutes on this question.

 Links You can revise ways in which the Nazis established a dictatorship on page 17.

Guided The Enabling Act of 1933 and the elimination of

political opposition were both important reasons that the

Nazis were able to establish a dictatorship. However, I think

the more important reason was

....

....

....

....

....

....

....

....

....

....

....

....

....

....

....

....

....

....

....

....

....

In your opening paragraph, come to a **judgement** about which reason was more important.

Remember that you need to concentrate equally on giving information to show what you know about the events in the bullet points **and** analysing and explaining how they led to the establishment of the dictatorship.

Examine **both** of the bullet points given in the question and give detailed information on both of them throughout your answer.

You don't need to include any other reasons besides those given in the bullet points. You just need to **evaluate** the two given reasons.

Practice

Use this page to continue your answer to Question 6.

....

....

....

....

....

....

....

....

....

....

....

....

....

....

....

....

....

....

....

....

....

....

....

....

....

....

....

⬅ If possible, you should also show how the two reasons given in the bullet points are **connected** to each other. For example, the Enabling Act allowed Hitler and the Reich Cabinet to propose and pass laws without the Reichstag. This made it possible to pass the laws that helped to eliminate the political opposition.

⬅ Try to build an argument throughout the whole essay.

ANSWERS

SUBJECT CONTENT
Germany and the growth of democracy

1. Ruling Germany

Kaiser: Emperor, head of state and government in Germany
Reichstag: Parliament
Chancellor: Chief Minister (or Prime Minister)
Prussia: the largest, wealthiest and most influential of the states that combined to become Germany in 1871.
Militarism: the belief in the importance of a country having strong armed forces.

2. Kaiser Wilhelm II

(a) The army generals had considerable influence on Kaiser Wilhelm II, who frequently sought and heeded their advice.

(b) The Reichstag had little influence on Kaiser Wilhelm II but he had to take some notice of it as he needed its consent to pass legislation.

(c) Kaiser Wilhelm II's first Chancellor, Caprivi, undertook some measures Wilhelm II didn't like, so he dismissed Caprivi and ensured that other Chancellors were willing to do what he wanted. They therefore had little influence on Wilhelm II.

3. Industrialisation and socialism

Answers might include the following:
- Industrialisation created poor living and working conditions which the Kaiser was expected to solve. His governments passed social reforms to try and counter this.
- Industrialisation caused rapid urbanisation and therefore problems of poor living conditions – some social reforms were passed to try and counter this.
- Industrialisation needed high immigration rates to work in the new industries but this created social problems.
- Industrialisation widened the gap between the rich and the poor. To try and counter this some welfare provisions were put in place.
- Industrialisation caused a growth in socialism and the rise of the Social Democratic Party, which gained increasing numbers of votes in the

Reichstag. This caused the Kaiser problems as he needed the Reichstag to pass legislation and the SPD often tried to block laws, as with the Navy Laws.

4. The Navy Laws

Reasons why many Germans approved of the Navy Laws could include:
- It was patriotic and nationalist to support the Navy Laws as the Kaiser wanted.
- They would lead to further industrial growth and employment.
- Germany's empire (both current and future) would need protecting.
- A navy was necessary to increase Germany's empire.
- Having a large navy would be a great symbol of Germany's power in the world and rival the power of Britain.

Reasons why some were opposed to the Navy Laws could include:
- The effects of the Navy Laws would cost a huge amount of money.
- Some thought the focus should be on building up the army rather than the navy.
- Some worried about the rivalry with Britain that was developing.

5. The difficulties of ruling Germany

The rise of socialism would probably have worried Kaiser Wilhelm II the most. Socialists had a desire for a more equal society where power, land and business were shared between everyone. This was a direct contrast to the Kaiser's strong belief that it was his destiny to rule over everyone else. The SPD attracted increasing support. As well as delaying the Kaiser's legislation from being passed, it would also have shown that socialism was becoming more popular.

6. War weariness and economic problems

1 Food shortages. Many Germans were suffering terribly and, by the middle of 1918, many were malnourished.

2 Shortages of other essentials such as medicines (affecting health) and raw materials (affecting production and jobs).

3 Wages had been restricted so remained low. This was a problem because of inflation: the German mark was worth much less than it had been, so the people could buy less than before.

7. Germany's defeat

Any three from the following:
- US President Wilson wanted Germany to become a democracy and therefore demanded the abdication of the Kaiser before peace negotiations would begin.
- The army leaders who had effectively been running Germany in the summer of 1918 realised the war was lost (at least partly due to their own actions) and left the Kaiser to take the blame, refusing to support him. Without the support of the army leaders it would be almost impossible for the Kaiser to continue.
- The Kaiser had completely lost control of the military – naval mutinies and so on.
- The Kaiser had lost control of Germany – uprisings in many towns and cities had left many workers and soldiers in charge rather than the Kaiser's officials.
- The Kaiser had lost the support of the Reichstag.

8. Post-war problems

- Pensions became worthless. Those affected included the elderly and war widows.
- Savings became worthless. Those affected included the middle-classes because they were more likely to have savings. However, people with mortgages and loans benefited, as they could now pay them off. Businesses with loans also benefited, and some of these businesses took over other businesses that were struggling.
- Fixed rents became cheaper. Those who benefited included people who rented rooms or shops.
- Wages didn't rise as quickly as inflation. This reduced the value of workers' wages.
- Higher price of food. This benefited farmers, because they were paid higher sums for their products.
- The price of raw materials and parts rose so some businesses went bankrupt. This affected workers and the people who owned the businesses.

9. The Weimar government

Answers could include any three from the following:
- In 1890 the head of state was the Kaiser, a hereditary monarch. In 1919, the head of state was an elected president.

- The head of state in 1919 had far less power than the Kaiser had had.
- In 1919 the Reichstag was less powerful than the Bundesrat had been, and was an elected body.
- In 1890 the the Reichstag was more powerful than the Bundesrat; in 1919 it had far more and was the more important of the two houses of parliament.
- The electorate in 1890 was all men over 25 years. In 1919 it was all men and women of 21 years and over.

10. Change and unrest, 1919–23

The Freikorps were sent by the Weimar government to put down the Spartacist Revolt in Berlin, in 1919. This led to street fighting. In March 1920, the Freikorps marched on Berlin in protest, fearing that they would become unemployed. The government asked the army to stop the Freikorps but the head of the army refused and the Weimar government fled from Berlin. The Freikorps put a nationalist politician, Dr Kapp, in charge. The government persuaded the trade unions to go on strike. This caused chaos and made it impossible for Kapp to run Germany, so he fled and the Weimar government returned to Berlin.

11. Economic developments, 1924–29

The crisis of 1923 was resolved in the short term but Germany was now very reliant on American loans. The problem with this was that, if in the future America faced economic difficulties, Germany would experience the knock-on effect. Also, extreme political parties were against paying any reparations, which meant they were very hostile and wanted the democratic system to fail.

12. International agreements

Ways in which international agreements helped German recovery might include:
- They reduced reparations payments or made them more manageable, which helped the German economy.
- They gave German businesses loans, which significantly helped them to recover – increasing employment and prosperity.
- They increased the popularity of the Weimar Republic and moderate political parties.
- They helped to decrease support for extremist parties, therefore helping political stability (which also helped economically).
- They improved Germany's international position which in turn boosted the popularity of the government and helped economically.

Ways in which international agreements did not help or were unpopular might include:
- Economic recovery was not universal as some sectors – for example, agriculture – did not benefit from the international agreements and did not experience economic growth.
- Some aspects of the international agreements were unpopular – for example, some disliked the fact there were still reparations being paid at all, some disliked new borders with France, and so on.
- They did not reverse the Treaty of Versailles, which many Germans hated.
- Although they helped economic recovery, they ensured the recovery was dependent on American loans which made the recovery fragile.
- Although reducing support for extremism, there was still some support for extremist parties and they did not disappear completely.

13. Weimar culture

Art, cinema and architecture in Weimar Germany all challenged traditional ideas. They each experimented with new techniques, styles and materials, and were all touched by Expressionism, so the emotions and feelings generated were important.

Germany and the Depression

14. Growth of extremism, 1928–32

Any one from the following:
- As businesses reduced staff or closed completely, millions of people lost their jobs. Young people were particularly badly hit.
- Poverty increased hugely due to many people being unemployed, and the reductions made to unemployment benefit.
- The Weimar government and democracy itself became much weaker as the moderate parties in the Reichstag could not agree on how to tackle problems. The Chancellor had to bypass the Reichstag completely and ask the president to pass emergency laws.
- Support for extremist parties (the KPD and the Nazis) vastly increased as people became more disillusioned with the Weimar government and were attracted by the solutions to many of the economic problems the extremists offered.

15. Hitler's appeal

Any five from the following:
- After 1929, the Depression led to huge economic problems and hardship for many Germans. This led voters to support extremist parties that seemed to offer solutions.
- Many people were worried that the Depression would lead to a communist government. They therefore voted for the strongly anti-communist Nazi Party. Hitler promised to stand up to communism and offered alternative solutions to economic problems.
- The Weimar government was not able to solve the economic problems caused by the Depression. In fact it alienated its former voters by increasing taxes on the middle and upper classes and restricting unemployment benefit. Voters were looking for an alternative to the moderate political parties that didn't seem to have the answers.
- The Nazis portrayed themselves as very strong and organised – strong leadership with Hitler and a strong paramilitary force (the SA) to control disorder.
- The appeal of Hitler – he was popular due to his rousing speeches and messages that appealed to many different types of German. He also came across as strong and decisive, in contrast to Weimar politicians.
- Some very wealthy businessmen supported the Nazis and financed their election campaigns. This meant the Nazis could afford a lot of publicity material and fly Hitler all over Germany to put the party's message across.
- The Nazis campaigned very effectively to appeal to different sectors of German society, such as targeting business people by stating their anti-communist beliefs and saying they would solve the economic crisis.
- The SA sabotaged the opposition parties' election campaigns by disrupting meetings, destroying posters and intimidating candidates. This meant these parties received fewer votes than they would otherwise have done.

16. Hitler becomes Chancellor

Any two from the following:
- Most laws were passed by presidential decree rather than getting the agreement of the Reichstag.
- Chancellors were appointed who were not members of the Reichstag. This was allowed but undermined the Reichstag.

- Proportional representation meant that governments were always coalitions. In the time of crisis brought on by the Depression, a government couldn't be formed as the parties in the Reichstag all disagreed with each other.
- The 'Cabinet of Barons' – Papen's government were mostly not elected officials but business leaders and so on.
- Hindenburg mostly ruled by decree using his advisers, including army officials and friends rather than the Reichstag.

17. Removing opposition

The Reichstag fire was blamed on the communists. This gave the Nazis a reason for arresting communists, therefore ridding themselves of major political opponents. However, the fire actually enabled Hitler to go further than this because he issued the Decree for the Protection of the People and the State, which allowed him to get rid of more political opponents. The fire was presented as an attack on the political system and whole German government. It was therefore necessary to protect Germany from further attacks. This allowed Hitler to pass the Enabling Act, which gave him the power to pass laws without the approval of the Reichstag.

18. Hitler becomes Führer

The Communist Party was accused of starting the Reichstag fire in February 1933, in an attempt to bring down the government.

↓

This gave Hitler the opportunity to arrest 4,000 communists and issue a Decree for the Protection of the People and the State. This gave him the power to imprison other political opponents and ban the newspapers of opposition parties.

↓

Hitler used force to prevent the Communists taking up their Reichstag seats after the March 1933 election. This meant the Nazis had a majority and could therefore pass the legislation Hitler wanted.

↓

The Enabling Act of 1933 essentially ensured Germany was no longer a democracy, but that Hitler would propose new laws and the Reich Cabinet would pass them.

↓   ↓   ↓

This led to the banning of the Social Democratic Party in June, and the Centre Party and Nationalist Party dissolved before they were banned. Finally the Law against the Formation of New Parties banned any political party except the Nazis.	Regional parliaments were reorganised with Nazi majorities and then banned.	Trade unions were banned and officials were arrested. The Enabling Act of 1933 essentially ensured Germany was no longer a democracy, but that Hitler would propose new laws and the Reich Cabinet would pass them.

On 30 June, Hitler orchestrated the Night of the Long Knives, in which people posing potential opposition within the Nazi party were murdered.

↓

In August, after the death of Hindenburg, Hitler passed a law to merge the Chancellor and President roles and create a new position as Führer. Finally he made the army swear a personal oath of allegiance to him, rather than to the country.

The experiences of Germans under the Nazis

19. Employment

Any three (or more) from the following:
- Setting up public works programmes, which created jobs.
- Giving loans, subsidies and tax relief to companies so they could employ more people.
- Increasing trade and production, which created more jobs.
- Rearmament increased jobs.
- Conscription took some people out of employment figures, plus the army expanded.
- National Labour Service was compulsory and took people out of the figures.
- People in concentration camps weren't counted in the figures.
- Many Jews and women were forced to give up their jobs.

20. Nazi economic policies

The Four-Year Plan can be seen as a success in the following ways (any three):
- Even though targets weren't met, large-scale rearmament did occur.
- Rearmament helped to reduce unemployment.
- Some businesses benefitted hugely through rearmament.
- Some farmers benefitted from the drive for self-sufficiency.
- Many Germans believed the propaganda that said Germany was becoming more self-sufficient.

The Four-Year Plan can be seen as a failure in the following ways (any three):
- Targets for industrial production were not met.
- Food production only grew slightly so imports were still needed. This led to food shortages.
- In 1939 Germany still depended on imports for one-third of raw materials.

- Scientists had little success finding substitutes for raw materials that Germany did not have.

21. The impact of war
Any three from the following:
- Thousands were killed or injured by bombs.
- Bombs destroyed people's properties and businesses.
- More and more men were conscripted into the armed forces.
- Working men were conscripted into war work.
- More women were conscripted into work.
- Food and other items were rationed from the start of the war, so it could be difficult to get luxuries or certain products.
- As the war increased, there were more and more food shortages. These shortages especially affected the poor, who could not afford to buy on the black market.
- Eastern Germans in particular became refugees as they fled from the advancing Russian armies after 1944.

22. Impact on women
Any three from the following:
- Using propaganda to show women the importance of having children and their role in the Third Reich.
- Reforming education so that girls were focused on looking after the home and children rather than academic subjects.
- Using financial incentives – letting couples off repaying one-quarter of their marriage loan for each child they had, and giving women monthly payments to help raise their children.
- Raising the profile of women who had lots of children, through giving them medals and so on.
- Using the law to prevent women from having careers, such as banning women from the professions, banning grammar schools which prepared girls for university.

23. Young people and youth groups
Answers might include the following:
- To create proud Germans who supported a strong, independent Germany – singing patriotic songs; taking part in marches and rallies.
- To make sure the next generation would be loyal supporters of the Nazi Party and to believe in Nazi policies – learning about Hitler and Nazi policies; learning about racial superiority; taking part in Nazi rallies and marches.
- To help children be strong and healthy so they would produce many children – emphasis on sport and physical activity during youth groups.
- To prepare girls for their future lives as wives, mothers and housekeepers – separate youth groups for boys and girls; focus on cookery, housework, needlework, babies and childcare.
- To prepare boys for their future lives as soldiers and workers – military style camps and activities such as shooting emphasis on physical fitness.

24. Impact of education on the young
The Nazis had different aims for boys and girls. They wanted boys to be taught skills that would be useful in their future career as soldiers; girls were taught things that were useful for becoming mothers and looking after the home.

25. Churches and religion
Ways that the Churches cooperated:
- The Catholic Church signed the concordat.
- The Reich Church supported the Nazis and its members called themselves German Christians.
- Reich churches were well attended.
Ways that the Churches resisted:
- In 1937, the Pope issued 'With Burning Anxiety', which criticised the Nazis.
- Some individuals spoke out and were punished.
- In 1934, some Protestants broke away and set up the Confessional Church to secure more independence from Nazi control.

26. Aryan ideas
The Nazis considered people from several groups to be 'undesirable', as they thought they were biologically impure, not contributing enough to society or behaving in any ways they thought unacceptable. Certain 'races' of people were even identified as 'sub-human' (Untermenschen) or 'racially inferior' to Aryans. These groups included:
- Jewish people
- Roma ('gypsies')
- Slavs.

27. Racial policy and persecution
The Nazis described Roma people as Untermenschen and 'inferior' to the Aryan ideal. After 1933, the Nazis began to arrest Roma and place them in concentration camps. After the Nuremberg Laws were passed in 1935, Roma were no longer allowed to marry or have sex with Aryans. As the decade wore on, the treatment of Roma became harsher and their freedoms curtailed. In 1936 some were sent to special camps. In 1938, there were laws passed to prevent any Roma travelling and, also, they had to be registered. In 1939 they were threatened with deportation, which began in 1940–41 when some Roma were sent to labour camps or Jewish ghettos in Poland. In 1942 Himmler ordered the deportation of all Roma from Germany to concentration camps in Poland. Many were sent to Auschwitz. Over 200 000 were killed.

28. Jewish persecution
Kristallnacht marked a turning point because it was the first time that widespread destruction was used to destroy Jewish property and violence was used to attack and kill many Jews. Before this time persecution was generally economic and social.

29. The 'Final Solution'
Any three from the following:
- Before the war, severely disabled people were sterilised. During the war thousands were killed in the T4 programme.
- Severely disabled babies and children were killed only after the war started.
- Roma people were deported to camps or ghettos in Poland during the war. Previously, they remained in Germany.
- Jews were completely separated from gentiles in ghettos in towns and cities in Eastern Europe after the start of the war.
- Mass killing of Jews began. Jews were killed by Einsatzgruppen units, which followed the main German army after the invasion of Russia.
- Death camps killed millions of Jews by gassing them – the 'Final Solution'.

30. Propaganda and censorship
Any five (or more) from: posters, radio, films, newsreels, newspapers, sport, rallies and parades, art.

31. Nazi culture
Any three examples from the following:
- Anything glorifying the military – stories/films of war heroics, marching music, paintings of military heroes.
- Large, traditional buildings in the style of Ancient Rome/Greece.
- Traditional classical music by German composers – Beethoven, Bach, Mozart.
- Richard Wagner's music.
- Anything glorifying family life – paintings of large, traditional Aryan families; family stories and so on.
- Literature or film that demonised groups that the Nazis hated, including Jews and Communists.

- Images, films, books celebrating Hitler.
- Stories, paintings, and so on, of traditional German (Aryan) heroes from the past.

32. The police state

Repression was mainly used through the Gestapo and SS. Anyone who opposed the Nazis or behaved in a way that was not deemed acceptable could be arrested by the Gestapo and SS at any time. Both the SS and Gestapo operated above the law, so used violence and torture. Many people who opposed or criticised the Nazis 'disappeared'. A major weapon of repression was the concentration camp system where people were placed instead of a conventional prison. The police state also ensured there was little opposition as people were so afraid of the concentration camps, SS and the Gestapo, that they said and did nothing against the regime.

33. Opposition, 1933–39

Opposition groups such as the Edelweiss Pirates and Swing Youth were not large. There were only approximately 2,000 Edelweiss Pirates across the whole of Germany by 1939. These groups were also not political and offered no serious threat to the Nazi regime before the outbreak of the Second World War.

34. Opposition, 1939–45

White Rose Group:
- Created and distributed leaflets telling people about Nazi atrocities and trying to make more people openly resist them.
- They were very effectively dealt with – all the leaders and some other members were caught and executed.

Edelweiss Pirates:
- Spread Allied propaganda, sheltered army deserters, attacked members of the Hitler Youth and tried (and succeeded) in killing some Nazi officials.
- Those caught were dealt with harshly but many were not caught so the Nazis didn't deal that effectively with this group although they were still fairly small scale and didn't pose a huge threat.

Swing Youth:
- More Swing Youth groups emerged in many German cities. They resisted mainly through listening to jazz and behaving in ways the Nazis deemed unsuitable. They did become more political during the war and some spoke out against the regime.
- They were not considered a massive threat to the Nazis and therefore didn't need to be effectively dealt with. However, more members were

sent to concentration camps than previously.

Army opposition:
- There were several plots to try and kill Hitler, the July Plot of 1944 nearly succeeded.
- Opposition from the army was taken extremely seriously by the regime. However, it was not dealt with that effectively until, for example, the July Plot had taken place (it was not discovered earlier). To prevent further opposition from the army it was effectively placed under SS control from July 1944 which did effectively restrict members of the army from resisting the regime.

PRACTICE
45. Practice

1 Interpretations A and B both discuss Nazi tactics and support but offer different views. Evans claims Nazi support resulted from its propaganda tactics. He argues that the Nazis were skilled at targeting different interest groups with specific messages that appealed to them and that this led to their support growing. On the other hand, Kershaw claims that it was Hitler himself that appealed to many people and led to growing support. He speaks of 'victims of the Hitler Myth' and the 'growing feeling' that Hitler was an extraordinary leader.

46. Practice

2 Interpretations A and B offer different views about Nazi tactics and support because they focus on different aspects of the issues involved. In Interpretation B, Kershaw, in his work on the 'Hitler Myth', seeks to explain Hitler's popularity in terms of Hitler's ability to create a 'Führer cult'. Kershaw's perspective is concerned with the impact of Hitler's very personal appeal, even on those who were not natural Nazi supporters. Evans, on the other hand, is looking more widely at reasons and his focus is more on the impact of the Nazi tactics, and how they led to increased support rather than focusing just on Hitler.

47. Practice

3 Either interpretation could be found more convincing.
- **To support Interpretation A:** I find Interpretation A more convincing because it is true that the Nazis were skilled at targeting a range of different groups and adjusting their message accordingly. For example, their slogans included 'work and

bread' to attract working-class votes. On the other hand, they campaigned to get rid of the Treaty of Versailles to appeal to nationalist-minded voters who still resented the outcome of the First World War. Evans argues that the Nazis adapted their message during the course of the economic depression in order to capitalise on the bad effects the crisis was having on the German people. This is certainly true as many Germans were suffering badly due to the Depression and the Nazi promised to create employment and solve the economic problems. Kershaw doesn't mention the power of Nazi propaganda or the targeting of groups, which was an important factor in the Nazi's appeal.
- **To support Interpretation B:** I find Interpretation B more convincing because, as Kershaw argues, Hitler managed to create a personality cult. Kershaw claims that even those German voters who did not share Hitler's 'sentiments' accepted that he was not like any ordinary politician. Kershaw's arguments about the significance of the 'Hitler Myth' helps explain the dramatic increases in the Nazi share of the vote in the 1932 election as he was indeed presented as superhuman and the saviour of the German people. Hitler himself was the focus of much Nazi propaganda.

The best answers will explain that both interpretations are true because Hitler and the propaganda worked side by side. Hitler and Goebbels understood that propaganda needed to be targeted at specific audiences and this was vital in their increased popularity at elections. Hitler himself adapted his message for different audiences and interest groups, like the young or workers.

49. Practice

4 Any two from the following:
- The rationing system was no longer working so there were severe food shortages. People were dependent on the black market but only some could afford this. Others had to scavenge and beg for food. More food was available in rural areas.
- More and more Germans had been conscripted into work to try to cope with labour shortages. Those Germans in concentration or labour camps were forced to work hard with few breaks or rations.

- Bombing had already destroyed homes and businesses in many towns and cities so many people were homeless and without employment.
- Bombing was continuing so many people were afraid. Many relocated or sent their children to rural areas where it was safer.
- Many people had been injured in bombing so were in pain but medicines and other medical equipment were in short supply. Also most doctors were with the army by this stage so there were few medical professionals to look after the injured.
- Germans in eastern areas or those living in Poland, East Prussia and Czechoslovakia became refugees – leaving their homes and going east, fleeing the invading Russian armies. They had few possessions, were homeless and subject to the same food shortages as other Germans.
- Towns and cities in western areas were flooded with refugees – this impacted the local population, as they had to find shelter for these people as well as share their meagre food supplies.

50. Practice

5 Answers could include the following:
- Rationing meant people were less able to buy the food and other consumer goods they wanted to buy from August 1939. This would have affected people's diets and their daily lives as, for example, they would have had to spend more time queuing to buy goods. It would have also affected other aspects of life such as travel, as fuel was rationed. As clothing was rationed, (mostly) women spent more time making and mending clothes and swapping second-hand clothing. After 1943, rations were reduced so people would have been more affected. By 1945, there were serious shortages of food and other essentials. Many people struggled to buy food and their health therefore suffered. Some had to scavenge for food while others relied on the black market.
- Many men were conscripted into the armed forces so would have had to leave home. This would have affected their families and friends left behind both emotionally, through fear and worry, and practically, as other people had to do the chores and tasks the man would do.

- Many men had to change jobs even if they weren't conscripted into the forces, especially from 1943 when non-essential war businesses were closed down so everyone could focus on producing the armaments and military equipment needed for the war, or food or other essentials. More women were conscripted into work from 1943 for the same reason.
- Allied bombing meant many Germans' homes and businesses were seriously damaged, leaving some people homeless. Up to 500 000 were killed and 750 000 injured in bombing raids. Bombing also damaged food supplies and supplies of other essential goods, water supplies, electricity and transport, which would all have had a profound effect on people living in bombed cities.
- Many Germans left their homes and became refugees, either from the town to the countryside, which was less likely to be bombed, or, after July 1944, to escape the invading Soviet Red Army.

52. Practice

6 Either can be argued to be the more important reason.
- Enabling Act: The Enabling Act of 1933 and the elimination of political opposition were both important reasons that the Nazis were able to establish a dictatorship. However, I think the more important reason was the Enabling Act. The Reichstag fire of 27 February 1933 led to the Enabling Act, as Hitler used the fire to stir up more fear of communists and to call another election. Although the Nazis still didn't win a majority in the election of March 1933, they effectively had a majority because they used emergency powers to prevent the communists taking the seats that they had won. This and the use of the SA to intimidate non-Nazi members of the Reichstag meant that the Nazis were able to convincingly pass the Enabling Act. Hitler presented the Act as essential because of the emergency situation caused by the Reichstag fire. The Act effectively destroyed democracy in Germany, as the Reichstag was no longer needed to pass laws and the German constitution could be overruled. The Act meant that only Hitler could propose new laws and only the Reich Cabinet

could pass them. The Act was therefore vital in destroying democracy in Germany, which was the main means of establishing a dictatorship. Without the Act, the Nazis would still have had to rely on the Reichstag to pass legislation, which would mean the Reichstag could prevent the Nazis from doing all the things they wanted. Eliminating political opposition was of secondary importance to this because there wasn't a democratic system in which other parties could be elected anyway.
- Elimination of political opposition: The Enabling Act of 1933 and the elimination of political opposition were both important reasons that the Nazis were able to establish a dictatorship. However, I think the more important reason was the elimination of political opposition. Gradually, different political parties were eliminated by different methods. Hitler used the panic caused by the Reichstag fire to arrest thousands of communists. Most of them were placed in concentration camps and most who were left fled Germany. In May 1933, the offices of other political parties were confiscated. They also confiscated the other parties' funds so they didn't have access to finance to operate. Then a series of laws was passed: the SPD was banned as a party; the Law against the Formation of New Parties ensured that no other political parties would be appearing. Members of the Centre Party and German Nationalist Party were so afraid that they dissolved the parties before they could be banned or arrested. Eliminating political opposition was vital as it effectively ended public debate of Nazi policies, therefore allowing those policies to take place. Even though the Enabling Act ensured that there was no Reichstag and no democracy, banning political parties meant it was extremely unlikely that democracy would be coming back.
The two things are connected as both were needed to ensure that only Nazi opinions were heard and Nazi policies could happen without political opposition preventing them.

Notes

Notes

Notes

Published by Pearson Education Limited, 80 Strand, London, WC2R 0RL.
www.pearsonschoolsandfecolleges.co.uk

Text and illustrations © Pearson Education Ltd 2017
Typeset and illustrated by Kamae Design
Produced by Out of House Publishing
Cover illustration by Eoin Coveney

The right of Kirsty Taylor to be identified as author of this work has been asserted by her in accordance with
the Copyright, Designs and Patents Act 1988.

Content written by Rob Bircher, Brian Dowse and Victoria Payne is included.

First published 2017

23
10 9 8 7 6

British Library Cataloguing in Publication Data
A catalogue record for this book is available from the British Library

ISBN 978 1 292 20476 5

Acknowledgements
The author and publisher would like to thank the following individuals and organisations for permission to
reproduce photographs:
Page 44 Used by permission of the publisher, History Today.
Pages 7–12, 14, 16, 17, 23, 24, 26, 30, 31, 55, 57 Revise Edexcel GCSE (9–1) History Weimar and Nazi Germany,
1918-39 Revision Guide and Workbook by Victoria Payne. Published by Pearson Education Limited © 2017,
pages 2, 4, 5, 6, 7, 9, 11, 12, 13, 14, 15, 17, 18, 20, 23, 28, 52, 54, 55 and Figure 1.1 on Page 24.

Note from the publisher
Pearson has robust editorial processes, including answer and fact checks, to ensure the accuracy of the content
in this publication, and every effort is made to ensure this publication is free of errors. We are, however, only
human, and occasionally errors do occur. Pearson is not liable for any misunderstandings that arise as a result of
errors in this publication, but it is our priority to ensure that the content is accurate. If you spot an error, please
do contact us at resourcescorrections@pearson.com so we can make sure it is corrected.